Out of
Women's
Experience

**CORWIN
PRESS**

The Corwin Press logo—a raven striding across an open book—represents the happy union of courage and learning. We are a professional-level publisher of books and journals for K-12 educators, and we are committed to creating and providing resources that embody these qualities. Corwin's motto is "Success for All Learners."

Out of Women's Experience

Creating Relational Leadership

Helen B. Regan
Gwen H. Brooks

CORWIN PRESS, INC.
A Sage Publications Company
Thousand Oaks, California

For information address:

Corwin Press, Inc.
2455 Teller Road
Thousand Oaks, California 91320

SAGE Publications Ltd.
6 Bonhill Street
London EC2A 4PU
United Kingdom

SAGE Publications India Pvt. Ltd.
M-32 Market
Greater Kailash I
New Delhi 110 048 India

Printed in the United States of America

Library of Congress Cataloging-in-Publication Data

Regan, Helen B.
    Out of women's experience: creating relational leadership / Helen
    B. Regan, Gwen H. Brooks.
            p. cm.
    Includes bibliographical references (pp. 109-112) and index.
    ISBN 0-8039-6233-9 (cloth : alk. paper). — ISBN 0-8039-6234-7
    (pbk. : alk. paper)
        1. Women school administrators—United States. 2. Educational
    leadership—United States. I. Brooks, Gwen H. II. Title.
    LB2831.82.R44   1995
    371.2'0082—dc20   95-12698

95 96 97 98 99 10 9 8 7 6 5 4 3 2 1

This book is printed on acid-free paper.

Corwin Production Editor: Diana E. Axelsen   Typesetter: Christina Hill

To
Peggy McIntosh,
whose vision
inspired
our own.

Contents

Foreword

This book has had an extended gestation. Figuratively, its first words were written over 20 years ago when a group of women who were school administrators formed the Northeast Coalition of Educational Leaders. Gwen Brooks and Helen Regan were among those East Coast women who gathered together to form an advocacy group for women school administrators. Simultaneously, on the West Coast I helped start Northwest Women in Educational Administration, and other groups were being formed in the Midwest, Southeast, and Southwest (Schmuck, 1995). Women in educational administration all over the country saw they were becoming extinct and formed political advocacy groups to regain administrative positions.

Since the 1970s the conditions have become somewhat more supportive for women administrators:

- The number and percentage of women administrators have increased (although women administrators at the superintendent level and principals of large high schools are still each below 20%).
- Sex discrimination was addressed legislatively through Title IX and other federal and state mandates.
- The stereotypical and negative attitudes of male administrators and professional organizations toward women's participation in leadership have become muted.

- Feminist scholarship on women's leadership has provided conceptual tools to understand how gender affects participation in school organizations.

Those 20 years of thinking and talking together are reflected in the book's purpose, which is to "describe the outcome and processes by which a group of women school administrators transformed their understanding of school leadership" (Chapter 1, this volume, p. 2). This was no small feat. Fortunately for historians and other women administrators, Gwen Brooks and Helen Regan decided to record their experiences and the experiences of nine other women administrators.

Twenty years ago those women became administrators by defying cultural norms for women and for school administrators. Brooks and Regan do not belabor stories of sex discrimination and the obstacles facing women in administration; those are already well recorded elsewhere (Schmuck, 1975, 1982; Shakeshaft, 1987). Instead they concentrate on what they learned about the practice of leadership.

Some women who entered administration used the models available to them: "We began by mimicking what we saw, learning to administer by modeling ourselves after the men around us, but harboring a secret belief that we would soon develop into better administrators than our models" (Chapter 2, this volume, p. 9). Not all women in educational administration, however, took such an exploratory position. Some continued to mimic the models available to them, and some eschewed anything to do with feminism and instead aspired to become "one of the boys" (Matthews, 1995; Schmuck & Schubert, 1995).

But the women described by Brooks and Regan continued their exploration; they discovered "points of rupture" (Chapter 2, this volume, p. 10), where they found themselves "insiders" in school organizations but still experienced being marginalized. Those women had enough chutzpah to resist socialization into the traditional administrative behavior and found their own way. Strong cultural pressures exist in school organizations to socialize teachers and administrators in the prevailing organizational norms, values, and beliefs; it is often difficult to remain true to oneself, to fit into the traditional organizational culture, and to find meaning (Hart, 1995).

The stories of the 11 women in this book reveal how they both resisted socialization into the prevailing culture and plumbed the depths of rupture. They acknowledged their own discomfort and the dissonance between the "expectations about how an administrator is expected to behave and what we ourselves felt was the way we should behave" (Chapter 2, this volume, p. 10).

What those women administrators have contributed to the practice and theory of education is a new conception of administrative practice—one that is *relational* rather than controlling. I especially like that their practice eschews the traditional concept of leadership as organizational position and managerial control. I have taught that effective leadership is relational, but in the past I have had difficulty finding texts that take this position. The authors argue, and I agree, that leadership may "also include the informal roles through which a person exerts influence on events and people" (Chapter 1, this volume, p. 7). Of course, principals lead, teachers lead, and students lead. If we view leadership as relational influence that can be performed by anyone, with or without legitimate authority, we move to a better understanding of how leadership must arise in democratic institutions. I think of leadership not as a person, place, or thing, but as a verb; leadership is the action of influence; it is relation, it does not exist by itself (Schmuck & Schmuck, 1992).

The authors speak of the importance of language. Traditional administrative language is the language of scientific management—span of control, hierarchy, authority, and division of labor. The new language is relational—caring, vision, collaboration, courage, intuition. These "unscientific" words are not new, but they are relatively new to administration theory. Brooks and Regan point out that even though the language is closely associated with maternal and female stereotypes; the concept of relation is not for women administrators only. I agree; both men and women can and do apply the concepts of relational leadership. I also believe that the increased presence of women administrators, as well as the emerging feminist scholarship, is corollary to the widening acceptance of the idea of leadership as relational (Noddings, 1992; Schmuck & Runkel, 1994; Sergiovanni,

1991). Women, such as those described in this book, may not have caused a rethinking of educational leadership, but if these explorations of the mind had not occurred in this setting and elsewhere, we might still be stuck in the traditional mind-set of leadership as legitimate authority and managerial control.

The authors go on to outline the concepts of relational leadership, giving specific examples, describing the political context of the Northeast Coalition of Educational Leaders, and presenting an historical and political context for women in school administration.

This book is grounded in the experiences of 11 women. It is political because it recognizes the power differentials between men and women in society and in schools. It is educational because it provides an alternative framework for thinking about leadership. It contributes to the literature on socialization by providing case examples of resistance to being socialized into the prevailing organization. I will use this book in a course I teach for new administrators called "The Ropes to Skip and the Ropes to Know." New administrators want to fit in, maintain their individual integrity, and find meaning; they each experience their own points of rupture. It takes courage and patience to resist the prevailing norms, and it takes strength to find and use relationship skills. Thank you, Gwen, Helen, Kathleen, Sarah, Carla, Nancy, Jennifer, Kristen, Jan, Susan, and Bethene, for sharing your affective and intellectual journey. It was an important journey to map.

PATRICIA A. SCHMUCK
Professor of Educational Administration
Lewis and Clark College
Portland, Oregon

References

Hart, Ann Weaver. (1995). Women ascending to leadership: The organizational sociali-
    zation of principals. In D. Dunlap & P. Schmuck (Eds.), *Women leading in education*
    (pp. 105-124). Albany: SUNY Press.
Matthews, Evelyn. (1995). Women in educational administration: Views of equity. In
    D. Dunlap & P. Schmuck (Eds.), *Women leading in education* (pp. 247-273). Albany:
    SUNY Press.
Noddings, Nel. (1992). *The challenge to care in schools.* New York: Teachers College Press.
Schmuck, Patricia. (1975). *Sex differentiation in public school administration.* Arlington,
    VA: National Council of Administrative Women in Education.
Schmuck, Patricia. (1982). *Women educators: Employees of schools in Western countries.*
    Albany: SUNY Press.
Schmuck, Patricia. (1995). Advocacy organizations for women school administrators,
    1977-1993. In D. Dunlap & P. Schmuck (Eds.), *Women leading in education* (pp.
    199-224). Albany: SUNY Press.
Schmuck, Patricia, & Schubert, Jane. (1995). Women principals' views on sex equity:
    Exploring issues of integration and information. In D. Dunlap & P. Schmuck
    (Eds.), *Women leading in education* (pp. 274-287). Albany: SUNY Press.
Schmuck, Richard, & Runkel, Philip. (1994). *Handbook of organization development for
    schools and colleges.* Chicago: Waveland Press.
Schmuck, Richard, & Schmuck, Patricia. (1992). *Group processes in the classroom.*
    Dubuque, IA: William C. Brown.
Sergiovanni, Thomas. (1991). *The principalship: A reflective practice perspective.* Boston:
    Allyn & Bacon.
Shakeshaft, Charol. (1987). *Women in educational administration.* Beverly Hills, CA:
    Sage/Corwin.

Preface

This book describes a model of leadership that is drawn out of the experience of women educational leaders. We are convinced that the qualities most women bring to leadership are inherently different from those practiced by most men, specifically as practiced in schools. We seek to broadcast the news that what we have come to call relational leadership is different in significant and positive ways from traditional leadership practices; and, also, that the attributes of relational leadership are accessible and valuable to women and men alike.

Moving beyond profiles of the backgrounds and careers of women in educational administration (see, for example, Biklen & Branigan, 1980; Edson, 1988; Shakeshaft, 1987), we describe how women conceptualize leadership and practice it in their roles as professional educators. Although the present state of our understanding of relational leadership does not allow us to extrapolate its meanings to other fields at this time, we believe the qualities inherent within it have significant implications for all leaders, women and men alike.

In Chapter 1, we begin with an introduction to the six ideas that have led to the writing of this book. In Chapter 2, we describe two metaphors of culture undergirding our assertion that the experience of women as school leaders has value and should be disseminated to all school leaders. In Chapters 3 and 4, we move to a discussion of the feminist attributes of leadership and to analysis of the practice of school leaders using the framework of the feminist attributes.

In Chapter 5, we describe the process of constructing knowledge from women's experience and the journey by which we came to understand the feminist attributes of leadership. We detail the history of a group of women school administrators who came together about 20 years ago and, through continuing relationships, have come to the ideas set forth in this book. Throughout the book, we illustrate the points under discussion by reference to the stories and experiences of members of our group, but in this chapter we describe the particular way in which our association, the Northeast Coalition of Educational Leaders (NECEL), nurtured the ideas that constitute this book.

In Chapter 6, we place the ideas we have conceptualized and articulated into a historical perspective, noting that, although we thought we were alone in formulating these ideas, in fact we stand in a long line of women who, for centuries, have analyzed the world using gender as a category of experience. It is only in retrospect that we have found both a theoretical framework within which to place our work and a historical tradition of which we now see ourselves as but one step. We conclude in Chapter 7 with a look at some of the possibilities for change initiated by both men and women through application and practice of relational leadership in schools.

Every chapter includes stories of our experiences told personally in the voice of their creators. In the text of the book, we use pseudonyms when telling personal stories, in the hope that the stories will echo the voices of other women who have experienced similar thoughts and experiences. In the few instances where the identity of the woman whose experiences are being described is essential to the story, we have so indicated, and in the acknowledgments that follow, we are pleased to list the names of all the women who have collaborated with us these many years to construct the understanding of women's experience as school leaders described here.

On the first page of the second chapter, Kathleen speaks. She will be joined on succeeding pages by Sarah, Carla, Nancy, Jennifer, Kristen, and Jan (all pseudonyms); Susan Villani, Bethene LeMahieu, and the authors, Gwen H. Brooks and Helen B. Regan, are identified by their real names. We are all educational administrators out of whose experience the ideas set forth in this book have developed, most especially, the central idea that knowledge about school leadership can and should be constructed out of women's experience.

This book has been a collaborative effort from its beginnings until the final copy. So complete a collaboration has it been that we, the authors, would find it impossible to separate the written word into "Helen wrote" or "Gwen wrote." The thoughts, feelings, and ideas interwoven throughout the book are the articulation of the relational knowing in which the women whom we acknowledge below have engaged over these past two decades. We thank all of the women who have contributed; those we can identify by name and those whose thoughts and actions are reflected in our words. We feel we must especially thank Betty Allen, Cynthia Dubea, Carol Harrington, Vickie Hornus, Josephine Kelleher, Susan Stevenson, and Susan Villani for their care, their support, and their participation.

The women listed below contributed to this book by participating in one or more of its phases—the Future Directions Project, the 1989 NECEL Board of Directors, and the Conversers Conference—and/or were authors of essays about their experience as school leaders:

Betty Allen	Vicki Hornus	Suzanne Ming
Paulie Brading	Josephine Kelleher	Linda Raines
Judith Deshaies	Bethene LeMahieu	Charlotte Rosen
Cynthia Dubea	Beverly Lydiard	Doris Smith
Carol Eaton	Janet Manning	Susan Villani
Jacqueline Forbes	Betsy McElvein	Marje VonOhlson
Carol Harrington	Joan McGee	Betty Waters

We extend very special thanks to Carol Witherell, whose thoughtful and complete critique of an earlier draft of the manuscript contributed significantly to its quality. Special thanks also to Gracia Alkema and the staff of Corwin Press for their belief in the value of our work and their very helpful and encouraging advice.

HELEN B. REGAN
GWEN H. BROOKS

About the Authors

Helen Brooks Regan is Professor of Education and Coordinator of the Secondary Certification Program at Connecticut College, New London, Connecticut. Previously, she served as a high school principal, assistant principal, and chemistry teacher, and she has also consulted widely in the fields of staff development and teacher assessment. Her education includes a Ph.D. in educational administration from the University of Connecticut, M.A.T. from Yale University, and B.A. from Randolph-Macon Woman's College. Reflecting her interests in the fields of school leadership, feminist theory and pedagogy, and teacher education, her recent publications include "In the Image of the Double Helix: A Reconstruction of Schooling" in *Women Leading in Education*, D. Dunlap and P. Schmuck (Eds.), 1995, and *Teacher: A New Definition and Model for Development and Evaluation*, with M. Anctil, C. Dubea, J. Hofmann, and R. Vaillancourt, 1992. She is also an elected member of the Board of Education in her hometown of Madison, Connecticut, where she lives with her husband, daughter, and stepdaughter.

Gwen Hoisington Brooks is Assistant Professor of Education at Connecticut College in New London, Connecticut. She earned B.A. and M.A. degrees at the University of Hartford and a Ph.D. at the

University of Connecticut, Storrs. She taught grades 5 through 12 for 15 years in the public schools of Manchester, Connecticut, and was an administrator there for 12 years in the junior and senior high schools before leaving to teach at Connecticut College. Her doctoral research was in the adult development of women educators, and her continuing interest is in women's issues. As an adjunct professor at the University of Connecticut, she taught a graduate course in learning research and learning styles and has lectured, consulted, and written about learning styles, learning research, and women's issues. She lives in Manchester, Connecticut, with her husband, George. They have two daughters, three grandchildren, and one great-grandson.

Patricia A. Schmuck is Professor of Educational Administration at Lewis and Clark College, Portland, Oregon. She first investigated the issues facing women administrators in 1974 in her Ph.D. dissertation, "Sex Differentiation in Public School Administration." She has since authored or coauthored many articles and five books on women in administration, including, most recently, *Women Leading in Education*, edited with Diane Dunlap.

1

Introduction

Women's Experience as School Leaders

During the past three decades, women have taken a leadership role in redefining aspects of our lives—work, family, sexuality, justice. Women have influenced how we define reality, conceive of knowledge, and exercise leadership. . . . Clearly, women have achieved tremendous changes in this time; yet there are few studies of women leaders who made this happen and of how they did so. What research exists rarely goes beyond the most visible spokeswomen, and little is known of the creative approaches to leadership that have been at the heart of this movement.

—Charlotte Bunch

Our book goes beyond a discussion of the most visible spokeswomen Charlotte Bunch writes about in the Foreword to *Women of Influence, Women of Vision* (Astin & Leland, 1991, p. xi). We write about the experiences of some of the few women in school leadership positions powerful enough to change the ways in which schools are administered. We consider what is known and understood about the ways women lead by describing both the outcomes and the processes by which a group of women school administrators transformed their understanding of school leadership over a period of 20 years. It is a book built on the assumption that schools as presently constituted are deeply flawed institutions for all groups: students, parents, teachers, and administrators. Our assumption takes us to the position that relational leadership can create an environment for change in schools that will benefit each of their constituencies.

We develop six ideas in the book. First, we assert that women's experience as school leaders has value and that knowledge constructed from this experience should be disseminated to men and women alike. Second, we identify and explore the double helix as a metaphor that expresses the essence of leadership grounded in women's experience. Third, we name and define five attributes of relational leadership: collaboration, caring, courage, intuition, and vision. Collectively, we call this set of qualities *the feminist attributes of leadership* to indicate their source in the specific experience of women. However, as we trust the book makes abundantly clear, these attributes can be learned and practiced by both women and men. Relational leadership is created in practice by the union of the feminist attributes with the traditional practices described in works such as those by Senge (1990), Peters and Waterman (1982), and Sergiovanni (1992). Throughout the book we will refer to traditional attributes as the *masculinist* attributes to signal their source in men's experience, in contrast to the *feminist* attributes, which have their source in women's experience.

Next, we illustrate how these attributes can be used to analyze effective leadership practices. Then, we describe and advocate a process for perpetuating the cycle of constructing knowledge out of women's (and men's) experience, applying it in the world, and using the experience gained to generate another iteration of the cycle. Finally, we identify a historical pattern of suppression and loss of knowledge constructed out of women's experience and argue that this pattern must be ended.

As we frame this model of relational leadership, we draw substantially from the traditions and language of feminism. In our opinion, the theoretical structure that most usefully supports and informs the analysis of women's experience as leaders lies in the field of feminist theory. Consequently, throughout the book, we have woven stories of leadership by the group of women whose experiences inspired this book with feminist scholarship that helps to bring meaning to them. Complete understanding of relational leadership, in a way analogous to the practice of relational leadership, requires a synthesis of the feminist and the masculinist intellectual traditions.

Our argument for a feminist perspective on leadership is not an argument against traditional male-based formulations of leadership. Our intent is to reveal a knowledge base about leadership not widely understood or practiced so that it can be considered along with what we already know and do as leaders. The authenticity of our approach is its grounding in the female experience, and it reflects what we know to be true of ourselves and others in our experiences as educational leaders. The result of the feminist perspective will lead to a synthesis transcending both the male and female knowledge bases.

This book is about bringing balance, or wholeness, to school leadership, a process we sense is occurring in other fields as more women gain leadership positions. Although we cannot extrapolate our experience to areas where we have little or no experience, our own reading and association with women in businesses and organizations lead us to believe their experience is similar to those we describe here. For example, in her interviews with female heads of organizations and presidents and chiefs of businesses, Helgesen (1990) found that they were concerned about relationships. Rather than considering interruptions disruptive, they viewed unscheduled tasks and meetings to be opportunities, and they kept themselves accessible, particularly to subordinates. Each of these women held a high-level, responsible position; each had to make many tough decisions. Yet she considered it important to be caring, to be involved, to take time to listen, and to build relationships with the people with whom she worked (p. 21).

As school administrators, we too have been in countless situations where it has been essential that we demonstrate how tough we can be. We can relate many incidents when our caring qualities have been sorely tested. But we have plenty of models about how to be tough. What we need are models of how to care, so that we can integrate both sets of attributes, focusing a greatly enhanced knowledge base on the intractable problems of school and the world. Relational leadership as we define it is a balanced practice that can inspire us all to find creative solutions we have not known enough to conceive, because, historically, we have brought only half the knowledge about leadership to the task. Complete explication of relational leadership, fully and richly described by stories from experience, will bring meaning to the concept. This lies in the future. Relational leadership is the creative integration of masculinist and feminist attributes of leadership. This book complements knowledge about the former with knowledge about the latter, pointing the way for men and women to collaborate on illuminating the meaning and implications of integrating these attributes in practice.

We hope this book will be read by both men and women, by scholars and practitioners. This hope has caused us to think deeply about the likely mind-set of our readers. For those familiar with feminist literature, probably mostly women and mostly scholars, certain uses of language will not be off-putting. However, for other readers less familiar with this literature, we anticipate certain responses to our use of language that could be barriers to hearing our meaning accurately. A note about language as related to gender therefore seems appropriate.

The Importance of Language

Smith (1990) refers to "the undernurtured language of woman's voice," quoting Gail Scott, who maintains that women develop language through an early attachment and ongoing relationship with their mothers while at the same time developing a "fathertongue" in their relationship to their fathers. The consequence of this is a split relationship between the language of the "undernurtured woman's voice" and another, one that we try to speak to bridge the gap in "a man's world" (p. 3).

We struggle with this split language. It takes courage to speak with the woman's voice in and to the man's world, but this is our project. We are concerned about the reception our words will receive. Will we be understood as we try to initiate a serious conversation about what can be learned about leadership from analysis of women's experience? Will we be believed when we say we want both men and women to join in this conversation? We are even concerned about the use of the word *feminist* in describing the attributes of relational leadership. Will we be trusted when we declare that this book is not about replacing a masculinist perspective with a feminist perspective, but rather a book about progress through synthesis of both? Despite these concerns, however, we insist, as does Spender (1987), that we must invest the language with our own authentic meanings. We will insist on the authenticity of our language and pay heed to Spender's wise words of caution that we do so without the use of imposition, control, or devaluation of others (p. 5).

A main purpose of this book is to describe the feminist attributes of leadership, which at the moment are primarily practiced by women and learned through their gender-specific experience of the world. We must use language to communicate with one another; therefore, we begin with the words we have, speaking in and through the voices of women, although these voices may differ from that of the fathertongue. In addition, we realize that certain words that we use throughout this book may confuse you, the reader, if we do not clearly communicate why we have chosen to use them as we have. The words *feminine* and *feminist* are two that may confuse; therefore, we offer a brief explanation of the way we have chosen to use each.

Feminine attributes such as nurturance, compassion, and care are culturally ascribed to women and are frequently connected to their social roles. Inherent in these attributes is the notion of being in second place and having a circumscribed sphere of action and influence in the world, which emanates from a proscribed life in the world of home and family. Feminine attributes are received from the culture. Feminist attributes, on the other hand, emanate from the active experience of women in the world and are named and claimed by women themselves. To restate, the essential difference in meaning, as we use the terms, is one of origin: Attributes ascribed to women without their active involvement we term feminine, whereas attributes actively defined and claimed by women themselves are termed feminist. Many, if not most, of the qualities of being feminine are subsumed under the qualities of being feminist; however, our notion of feminist connotes empowerment of women to self-define and to act in any and all arenas of the world as they choose.

Chip Wood (1991), a man working in the traditional woman's world of elementary education, writes that teaching needs to be infused with the "maternal values [of] caring, compassion, relationship, and collaboration" (p. 3). He maintains that if this were done, the hierarchical structure of school administration and the authoritarian structure of the traditional classroom would be transformed.

We believe that people practicing the feminist attributes of leadership do act on maternal values and can transform the structure of the education system, but we are hesitant to call such qualities maternal. The connotations of the word *maternal* are problematic in two senses. First, we know many men who infuse these values into their teaching and their administering (Chip Wood is probably one of these men), and so we resist use of a word that may suggest that this aspect of human life is accessible to women only (or men only, for that matter). Second, use of the term *maternal* might suggest that only women have the power to transform the hierarchical structure of school administration. How ironic that use of a woman-associated word can lead to an inference that only women as a class have the power to bring about a transformation. We do believe that increasing numbers of women in positions of school leadership will hasten transformation of that field, but we do not believe that only women can bring about change in school leadership.

Although we choose not to use the term *maternal* because its connotations may confuse rather than clarify our meaning, we must begin with existing language, which can become a bridge to new ideas and new understanding and, in turn, convey new meaning upon old language. We are mindful that using words with feminine connotations creates the risk that we will be misunderstood, trivialized, dismissed; however, we take that risk in order to gain authenticity for the language that defines relational leadership. Just as it takes courage for us to speak about relational leadership as a viable alternative to the traditionally accepted forms of leading, so too it will take intuition on your part to hear us accurately. The terms we use convey an essential point: the feminist attributes of caring, courage, vision, intuition, and collaboration exist in the practice of most women leaders as a function of their gender.

The choice of words with which to name the feminist attributes of relational leadership is also problematic. *Caring* and *intuition* are rich with feminine connotation, leading to the possibility that they will be dismissed as unworthy or irrelevant to the practice of leadership. *Collaboration* seems to be a word in transition, discussed widely enough in the recent leadership literature to be gaining credibility that it did not carry only a few years ago. Like collaboration, *vision*, as in "the vision thing" popularized by former President George Bush's campaign rhetoric, is gaining currency, but it is not yet clearly defined. *Courage* prompts masculine images of daring deeds of some sort, and so it is problematic in an opposite sense. How can courage be a feminist attribute? We wish to celebrate the contributions of women to leadership practice and theory, an affirmation that demands the use of words with feminine connotations despite the fact that the juxtaposition of feminine and leadership can be received as an oxymoron. Whatever prior images and meanings you bring to this book for these words—feminist, caring, courage, intuition, vision, and collaboration—we ask that you set them aside and that you remain open to their reinterpretation as you read and think.

One of our colleagues who contributed to this book suggests that we probably need a whole new lexicon to describe our emerging definition of leadership. This may well be so. Grumet, in her foreword to *Exiles and Communities: Teaching in the Patriarchal Wilderness* (Pagano, 1990), writes that Pagano's meditations on teaching "celebrate and perform our power to make new worlds out of old words. . . . we work to transform the performance and performers. We work to make new meanings of old words" (pp. viii, viv). We, too, want to make new worlds of old words and transform the performance and performers, particularly in schools, wherever they are located. We believe that people practicing relational leadership can begin this transformation.

And so we come to a word about leadership itself. We use the term *leadership* broadly to include all the formal roles covered by the field of educational administration, as well as the informal roles through which a person exerts influence on events and people in her/his work situation. One of the women in our book suggests that a leader is a person who acts from firmly held beliefs or a deeply held value system. Clearly, there is a disjuncture for those who hold formal leadership roles but do not act out of firmly held beliefs. Are these people true leaders? Although we accept as leaders those who influence others by acting from a deeply held value system, we're unsure at this moment how we regard the converse. We do believe, however, that as the feminist attributes of leadership become widely understood and practiced, the definition of leadership will change, either resolving this question or rendering it moot.

Finally, this book is a collaboration. We, the authors, have written the words, but we are only two of many who have conceived the ideas that the words convey. Our purpose has been to make audible the thoughts and voices of a group of women educational leaders about our conceptualization and practice of leadership. We believe that relational leadership is a new way of knowing and thinking about leadership. This new way of knowing is reflected in the comments of one of our colleagues who said, "It seems to me the place to move in the future is to talk about behaviors for all of us regardless of whether we were born male or female." This is a new way of knowing, talking about, and acting on behaviors for all, confirming and celebrating them through women's voices.

However, women speaking is only one half of the equation; leaders, men and women alike, must listen and respond, not because they have been forced to do so, but because they genuinely believe there is something to be learned by doing so. We must enter a dialogue about effective leadership in which neither the role of the speaker nor the role of the listener is prescribed by gender. We believe the feminist attributes of leadership are accessible to women and men, even though we gain understanding of them through analysis of women's experience. Naming these attributes, rendering them visible, and teaching others to use them will enrich the practice of leadership in noticeable ways. A dialogue about effective leadership in which neither the role of the speaker or listener is prescribed by gender can then begin.

2

Two Metaphors of Culture

Gender as a Category of Experience

When we were novice school administrators in the mid-1970s, our notions of school leadership were formed primarily from watching the administrators around us, all men. We began by mimicking what we saw, learning to administer by modeling ourselves after the men around us, but harboring a secret belief that we would soon develop into better administrators than our models.

As a high school teacher, Kathleen, observing the ways in which administrators went about their jobs remembers, "In my heart of hearts, I always thought I could do better." She particularly mentioned the isolation of the staff, and she was certain there were things that could be done to break down that isolation, although she wasn't sure what they were. Kathleen found a great deal of personal satisfaction as a teacher, but she tells today of how she saw a move into

---

AUTHORS' NOTE: Portions of this chapter were previously published in H. Regan, "Not for Women Only: School Administration as a Feminist Activity," *Teachers College Record, 91,* 565-577. They are reproduced here with permission of *Teachers College Record.*

administration as an opportunity to break through that isolation and to bring about other needed change.

Retrospectively, we can see that Kathleen understood the role of collaboration from the beginning of her career, but at this very early stage, more than 20 years ago, she simply sensed that the isolation in which she worked was inhibiting. In general, none of us could articulate these feelings we had, and so we conformed eagerly to the norms of administrative behavior around us. It would be two decades before we would comprehend the significance of stories such as this, bring them to voice, and situate them in a theoretical context.

As the mid-1970s turned into the mid-1980s, many of us had completed graduate programs in educational administration, where we had learned about practices such as Theory X and Theory Y, the clinical model of supervision, and the process-product literature on effective teaching. Significantly, we had also gained enough experience in our administrative roles to become somewhat introspective. We felt an inchoate tension between what we saw other administrators do, what we had been taught was the theory underlying administrative practice, and what we found ourselves doing on occasion. We were beginning to discover the point of rupture about which Smith writes (1987):

> Inquiry into the implications of a sociology of women begins from the discovery of a point of rupture in my/our experience as woman/women within the social forms of consciousness—the culture of ideology of our society—in relation to the world known otherwise, the world directly felt, sensed, responded to, prior to its social expression. From this starting point, the next step locates that experience in social relations organizing and determining precisely the disjuncture, the line of fault along which the consciousness of women must emerge. (p. 49)

At this early stage of our administrative experience, we were beginning to discover the point of rupture, the disjuncture between the expectations about how an administrator is expected to behave and what we ourselves felt was the way we should behave. We relate here two of our early experiences with this disjuncture, experiences that gradually led us toward conscious awareness and articulation of the values that led to this disjuncture.

Jennifer tells the story of a disciplinary encounter she had in her role as assistant principal.

> I had been having a bad day—one confrontation after another. By the time this young woman walked into my office, my patience was at an end, and before she had time to tell her side of the story, I launched into a tongue-lashing and banished her to the detention room. Within minutes, I knew I had treated her unjustly, and in a few more minutes, I knew I had to apologize to her. I found her in the detention room, took her out into the hall, and said, "I'm sorry. I had no right to treat you that way."
>
> She was dumbfounded. "No grown-up has ever apologized to me before," she said. The student served the modified detention that was justified, but the sullen anger was gone and when she moved away several months later, there had been no further incidents of misbehavior.

Jennifer goes on,

> My fellow administrators were appalled that I had apologized to a student. They told me I was ruining my credibility with the students, that I would get a reputation as a soft touch, and so on. I just shook my head. I knew that what was wrong was my unjust treatment and that what was right was acknowledging that mistake to the person I had hurt.

This is an early example of relational leadership, the quality of acting with care consistent with one's firmly held beliefs. We had not named this attribute at the time of this incident, but it is clearly an example of a time when a leader acts with care and the courage to respond in a way counter to the conventional wisdom of what administrators "should" do in a situation like this. In caring environments, apologies are not connected to power relations, in which the obligation to apologize is restricted to the less powerful.

Helen, who at that time held an assistant principal's position, was eagerly seeking her own principalship. She relates an event that forcibly brought into her consciousness the tension between the pre-vailing norms of administrative behavior and her own intuitive sense of leadership. She characterizes the incident as stunning and as one in which her responses clearly ran counter to her own firmly held beliefs. In the midst of her job search, she agreed to serve as the can-didate in a mock interview for a superintendency to be conducted by a panel of practicing superintendents at a conference sponsored by the Connecticut affiliate of the Northeast Coalition of Educational Leaders (NECEL). "Although somewhat daunted by the audience of 60 people seated for the event," she relates, "I nonetheless per-formed at my best; tough, assertive, fielding the superintendents' questions confidently. Many people complimented me at the end of the session."

The next day back in her school, she was approached by a teacher friend who had been in the audience. Somewhat tentatively, the friend said she had a few reactions to the session of the day before, but she wasn't sure Helen would want to hear them.

> I swallowed and asked her to go ahead. What followed was one of the most helpful critiques of my work I have ever received. My friend began by acknowledging that she assumed that my perfor-mance was just the sort of hard hitting most people looked for in a superintendent. But, she went on, the woman she had seen per-forming was really not the person she knew. Where, she asked, were the compassion, the empathy, the gentleness, the gift for collabo-ration, qualities she had seen me use skillfully time and again to soothe students, encourage teachers, console parents? I was thun-derstruck by her comments. My friend had told me that qualities I knew I had, and which I knew were essential to my competent performance as an administrator, were not obvious in an interview.

Upon reflecting on her friend's comments, Helen realized that she deliberately, albeit unconsciously, buried those qualities during interviews because she believed they would be held against her.

> They did not match my image of the tough administrator I thought all interview committees looked for, particularly when the candi-date seated in front of them was a small woman looking 5 to 8 years younger than her actual age. Yet on the job I drew on these qualities

daily. It appeared that I was portraying myself during interviews as a machine gun spewing bullets when in actuality one of the keys to my success as an administrator was my ability to reduce the number of occasions when anyone needed to spew bullets.

In her next interview, Helen consciously modified her style to portray a balance of what she called at the time both her "hard" and "soft" qualities. She worked persistently in that interview to convey the idea that she could be hard and soft simultaneously, that neither set of qualities excluded the other. She got that job, but in retrospect, she says, that outcome was of secondary significance. Of far more importance was the fact that her teacher friend had given her the gift of her "complete and therefore authentic self." Unbeknown to either of them at the time, that incident had also set in motion the process of naming what we now understand to be the feminist elements of administering. The point of rupture between our experiences as women and the world of school administration around us was illuminated, vivid and startling, demanding explanation.

The Broken Pyramid

In the mid-1980s, Helen had the great good fortune to hear Peggy McIntosh, of the Center for Research on Women at Wellesley College, describe a metaphor of culture that led to the first moment of new understanding about the role of women as school leaders. McIntosh conceptualizes our culture as a broken pyramid with a fault line running through the middle (see Figure 2.1) (McIntosh, 1983). The fault line of McIntosh's pyramid turned out to be collinear with the accumulating ruptures between our experiences as women school administrators and what we observed in the behaviors of the men around us.

The metaphor of the pyramid describes the essence of the role differentiation in our culture. The pyramid has a fault line running through it at the middle. Above the fault is the world that operates competitively in an either/or mode. Either people move up the pyramid and gain more wealth, status, and power or they don't. The movement of those going up by definition prescribes failure for

Figure 2.1. An Illustration of the Broken Pyramid
NOTE: Used by permission of Nancy McDonough.

others, because there is room for fewer and fewer as the pyramid narrows at the top. Whole segments of our society have this vertical structure, for example, the military, the church, the corporation, the schools. Mostly white males occupy this upper part of the pyramid, and the closer to the top, the more dominant their numbers.

Below the fault line lies a whole different world, inhabited primarily by women, people of color, and low-status white males. Its organization is horizontal and collaborative; it is cyclical and repetitive. Most of daily life takes place here: doing dishes, changing diapers, planting the fields, and teaching. These are tasks that, when done, must be done again, repetitively, cyclically. This is where caring, nurturing, relationship, and community building happen. It's a both/and world.

Ferguson (1984) says that women tend to experience themselves as continuous with others and that this relationship is neither based purely on self-interest nor is it purely altruistic and self-sacrificing. She goes on to say that the values of caretaking, nurturance, empathy, and connectedness that are structured in women's experience carry both great strengths and great weaknesses (p. 25). We suspect that one of the great weaknesses of these values is that women have not themselves valued them. Their exclusion from the status, personal wealth, and power of life above the fault has conveyed the powerful message that recognition and rewards come to those who practice above-the-fault values, a position from which most women have been excluded. This is clearly reflected in the comments of one of the subjects of a study about women's developmental patterns, which Gwen conducted for her doctoral research (Brooks, 1980).

> I have to have something to do that I feel is of value and I can't go out and just do volunteer work either. I have to have something to earn money—something that has meaning. It's the money, I guess, that puts a value on what I'm doing. It's just that society puts a value on it, too, and I think that's important. (p. 93)

It is only in recent years, when women have gained the recognition and rewards of the workplace, that they have begun to recognize that the below-the-fault values they bring with them have intrinsic meaning and worth and are empowering to themselves and those with whom they work.

When Helen first heard the broken pyramid metaphor, she says,

> I was overcome with a sense of meaning revealed. It helped me understand why I believed it so essential to administering to be hard and soft at the same time. It helped me understand why it felt so right when my friend urged that I reveal the compassionate, collaborative side of myself as administrator in addition to the decisive, assertive side. Hard, I now saw, was above the fault; soft was below the fault.

After her introduction to the concept of the broken pyramid, Helen stopped using hard and soft to describe the double set of qualities she regarded as essential to effective administering, using instead the language of the metaphor, describing the double set of qualities as the ability to behave in both either/or and both/and ways, thus enabling one to move with ease across the fault line of the pyramid. (Notice that either/or is now surrounded by both/and). She reflects,

> I saw myself as having a wholeness, a totality of human experience
> and wisdom upon which to draw as I did my job, that is inaccessible
> to people, generally men, who are restricted to life above the fault,
> and to people, generally women and people of color, who are re-
> stricted to life below the fault. (Regan, 1990a, p. 568)

This coming to her first personal understanding of the concept
of balance led her to share the concept with other colleagues and gave
us our first inkling that school leadership might be enriched by a
synthesis of below-the-fault attributes, generally known and practiced by women, and above-the-fault qualities, grounded in men's
experience, but taught to and learned by all women who become
successful school leaders. Looking back on her experiences, Helen
became aware that she had always revealed, perhaps even over-
stated, her hard, above-the-fault qualities because she recognized
them as the qualities named and therefore valued in the generally
above-the-fault world of school administration. She says,

> Initially, my soft, below-the-fault qualities were hidden, even from
> me, because they are unnamed and therefore invisible and deval-
> ued in school administration. My teacher friend had begun the pro-
> cess for me of naming my gifts rooted in life below the fault;
> McIntosh, through the broken pyramid metaphor, gave me the lens
> that brought my below-the-fault gifts into sharp focus, and that
> showed me they are gifts also possessed by others. I came to recog-
> nize that most if not all successful school administrators whom I
> knew were part of a special class of people whose success was
> grounded in the ease of their movement back and forth across the
> fault. Because there has been only a women's movement, encour-
> aging women to move above the fault, but no men's movement
> encouraging men to move below the fault, this special class of peo-
> ple is mostly, but not exclusively, women. (Regan, 1990a, p. 569)

The broken pyramid metaphor, which had such an effect on
Helen's understanding of feminine qualities, was the impetus for a
series of seminars with Peggy McIntosh and the NECEL Governing
Board (an experience discussed in Chapter 5), which brought us to
new understanding of the feminist attributes. It was the first language that seemed connected to our growing awareness that the way

we as women went about our work as school leaders didn't exactly follow the male model. This metaphor assuaged a slight sense of guilt we had (but of which we did not yet speak, even to one another) that perhaps we weren't doing these jobs exactly as we had been taught. The metaphor allowed us to speculate that maybe there wasn't anything wrong with us, but rather we were bringing some of our below-the-fault qualities of care and collaboration to our work as school leaders, and this was *good*. The metaphor of the broken pyramid and recognition of the line of fault led us to our next step, bringing to consciousness and naming the feminist attributes of leadership.

New Understanding: Implications of the Broken Pyramid

Our encounter with the broken pyramid metaphor as an expression of role differentiation in our culture allowed us to understand that gender is a category of experience. Men and women experience and interpret the world differently as a function of their different genders. If one accepts gender as a category of experience, then one must also accept that women and men may experience and interpret the role of school leadership differently. Our central thesis is exactly that, hence the main title of our book, *Out of Women's Experience*.

As stated earlier in this book, we began to explicate school leadership from the viewpoint of women, using stories arising out of the experiences of our colleagues and ourselves. However, accepting that gender is a category of experience does not mean that learning arising from the experiences of the other gender is inaccessible. If this were true, we would be in the ultimate state of existential alienation. We believe each gender can learn from the experiences of the other *if* the experiences of the other are articulated and disseminated widely. In fact, such a process is what most education is about: articulating and disseminating the learning arising from male experience and analysis. The body of knowledge that we learned in our graduate school educations about school administration derives essentially and exclusively from male-based experience (see Martin, 1985), because the overall experience and knowledge of women as a gender is devalued and hidden in our culture, and because, in particular, women have been excluded from positions of school leadership; their experience, therefore, is not available as a source of knowledge. The success many of us had in learning and applying male-based knowledge about school leadership was not in and of itself a bad thing. After all, about half the knowledge in the world is constructed out of male experience, and all people, men and women, should learn this knowledge, experiment with it in the role of leader, and become knowledgeable critics of it. Astin and Leland (1991) say that change occurs when you first see the problem, get a clear picture of it, and then mobilize others by organizing the collective effort to bring about desired change within the existing structure, not necessarily by overthrowing what is there but by working within it (p. 116). The dynamics of change they have identified is exactly the process we ourselves have experienced and the process that has led us to the subtitle of our book, *Creating Relational Leadership.*

The problem does not lie in women learning about school leadership through the perspective of men's experience but rather in being told and believing that *that's all the knowledge there is.* How false, how immoral this is, and what a loss to everyone, women and men alike. Just as we believe that all people, women and men, can learn from the experience and interpretation of experience of men, so too we believe that all people, women and men, can learn from the experience of women. Fundamental change in leadership will come about when we affirm the value of women's experience, integrate the above-the-fault and below-the-fault qualities that are necessary for ethical leadership, and apply our new knowledge to the administration of our schools (in this case); it is to be hoped that such leadership will be extended into the wider world. Relational leadership is a model that synthesizes the finer qualities of the masculinist and feminist perspectives and forms a new, stronger, and more balanced practice of leadership.

Ferguson (1984) says, "Feminist theory is not simply about women, although it is that; it is about the world, but seen from the usually ignored and devalued vantage point of women's experience" (p. xii). Here our project becomes part of the larger feminist project under way in the wider world: valuing, articulating, recovering, and disseminating the experience and knowledge of women so that it becomes a resource for all, not only in the relatively narrow field of school leadership but in all aspects of the human condition. Our specific contribution is in constructing knowledge about school leadership from a feminist perspective, and in so doing we share in the work of feminist scholars in all fields. By analyzing women's experience, we believe we have created new knowledge. This is a bold claim, of course, which must be verified by others. At the very least, however, the five attributes of caring, courage, collaboration, vision, and intuition fit our experiences. We accept them as names for things we do consciously and continuously, and which most, but not all, of the men around us do not do to the same degree, or in the same way. They are certainly not qualities we were taught formally in our educations, but we believe they are qualities that *should be taught* to all aspiring school leaders, women and men alike. Men may have more difficulty putting them into practice, because the values are rooted in life below the fault where very few men tread. However, that's not to say men cannot learn them and thus traverse the fault line as successful women school leaders have always done, although in the opposite direction.

Smith (1987) maintains that a sociology of women will be "contained and institutionalized" if its concepts are not articulated and linkages created beyond the "ruling apparatus." This linkage will, she says, give voice to women's experience and open to women the "forms and relations determining women's lives, and enlarging women's powers and capacities to organize in struggle against the oppression of women" (p. 225). We agree that a necessary first step is giving voice to women's experience, but it is only a first step. We are not content to rest there. In fact, we argue that a means to struggle against oppression of women is not only in creating a linkage outside and beyond the ruling apparatus but also, and perhaps more important, in speaking with courage of the value of women's experience and working consciously to disseminate its teaching to women and men alike.

The Double Helix: Two Strands

As our understanding of the value of women's experience grew and we accepted that gender is a category of experience, a more appropriate symbol was needed to convey a reconfigured world in which the experiences of each gender would be recognized and valued on their own merits; a metaphor that would convey the balance essential to relational leadership: that is, qualities above the fault (masculine) and below the fault (feminine).

Over the next several years, Helen reflected on the metaphor of the broken pyramid, struggling with the creation of language to describe its antithesis. The terms *hard* and *soft*, and even the improvement in clarity resulting from use of the terms *above* and *below* the fault, clearly oversimplified a very complex idea. The goal of her search was to convey the idea that attributes from each mode of life have value. To do so we must break out of the pyramidal thinking where top means more valuable and bottom means less valuable. We need a metaphor that conveys the idea we now understand to be the crux of feminist administering, that is, life can be lived on both sides of the fault line, necessitating movement across it depending on circumstances, which in turn is an expression of the idea that both *either/ or* and *both/and* behaviors are required for competent administering. Not surprisingly, her training as a chemist and her background in teaching science led Helen to a metaphor that seemed adequate to the task—the double helix.

The double helix is the molecule of life; it is the shape of DNA, the molecule encoding our genetic information (see Figure 2.2). Each separate strand of the double helix, winding around and around, is a special sequence of amino acids that determines the form of life. The strands are linked together by bridges of hydrogen bonds.

Symbolically, the double helix fits our notion of balance, each strand representing a different facet of life as it was in the pyramid. One strand embodies life above the fault, representing the necessity of choice; there are times when life is either/or. The other strand embodies life below the fault, representing the necessity of collaboration; there are times when life is both/and. The hydrogen bonds linking the strands together represent the necessary and frequent passage from one mode of life to the other. The strands are intertwined; neither is superior to the other, because neither is always more valuable than the other, and because it is not possible to live a fully human life on one strand alone.

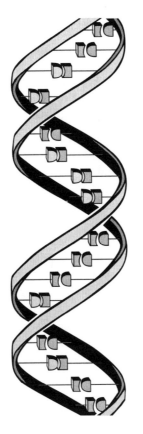

Figure 2.2. An Illustration of the Double Helix

The double helix now symbolizes and expresses the concept of relational administering for us. Its power lies in its inclusiveness, itself a feminist way of being, encompassing and legitimizing as it does both terms, the either/or and both/and ways of being, each strand depending on the other. As the antithesis of hierarchical organization, the double helix makes it clear that both genders need to move back and forth from the conceptualization of the world primarily associated with their gender to that associated with the other, and that both knowledge and praxis are incomplete if articulated through the perspective of one gender only. Furthermore, it makes clear that there are times when, although strength lies in wholeness, one strand must take precedence over the other. Here the fundamental values in the feminine strand are made plain; relational leaders collaborate and intuitively know when to make the shift from one strand to the other. In addition to literally shaping our lives, the double helix seems to describe our lives figuratively as well.

Articulation of the metaphor of the double helix as an inclusive expression of gender as a category of experience gave us the courage to seek actively for a language to describe the attributes (the amino acids) that constitute the feminine strand. The structure of the masculine strand is well-known to us all,[1] women as well as men, but the contributions of the feminine strand remain unknown, even to many of us who practice them daily. An unacceptable legacy of the dominant metaphor of role differentiation, the broken pyramid, is blindness and silence about the experiences of women and people of color. The double helix reconfigures the fault line so that the lines of the fault flex into a curvilinear structure, different in appearance from the linear structure of the pyramid. The metaphor of the double helix conveys that each side gains strength and equality of position, and that there is ease of movement between the two strands.

We offer the five feminist attributes as a first voicing of the structure of the feminine strand of the helix,fo in the hope that hearing will lead to seeing and ultimately that seeing will lead to changes in the practice of school leadership by all people.

The Double Helix: A Whole

Analysis of the feminine strand of the double helix is only one part of the possibility before us. The hydrogen bonds link the two strands of the double helix together into a functional whole that is different than either of its parts. The possibility before us is to integrate the male-based and female-based knowledge and practice of school leadership into an integral whole that will be different and more effective than either conceptualization of leadership alone.

We are not the first to see possibility in integration. Mary Parker Follett (1868-1933), out of her study of organizations in the early decades of this century, wrote and spoke extensively about the theory of integration. In her book, *Creative Experience*, written in 1924, she writes that the doctrine of circular response, which is involved in the theory of integration, is experience on every level, an interrelating that changes the terms of the relating as well as the relating itself; this gives us creative experience. "Creative experience is not compromise, but invention, in which two positions are integrated to form a new position which is neither of the two parts, but a new whole. This whole is not a product fixed immutably, but a 'whole a-making'" (p. 102). Integrative experience, Follett said, is always progressive (p. 106).

By describing the structure of the feminine strand of the double helix, we believe we are assisting a whole a-making. We notice that in our small worlds we have begun to create spaces where we actually see a new whole a-making. Interrelating our experiences as school leaders trained in traditional methods of school administration, with the attributes that are a fundamental part of our feminine selves has in subtle and not so subtle ways altered the terms of our relating to our roles as leaders and our relationships with those with whom we interact in those roles.

Kathleen, as the only woman in the superintendent's group in her area, realizes that her influence is transforming that group from one "where everyone is a star and God forbid that you should share a good idea," to a group where there is a new premium on sharing good ideas, particularly at this time when sharing ideas might assist with the problems of the struggling urban school district in the area adjacent to the affluent area in which she works. Faced with the task of changing the behavior of a group of men who had been conducting themselves in the same modes of behavior for umpteen years, Kathleen said,

> One of the things I've been complaining about since I've been there (and I think constructively) is how we can frame our group differently so we can share and collaborate as opposed to, "we have an agenda and it's the same four items every time." I'm a little tired of looking at it; I don't have to look at it, I already know what it is. Don't we have other needs?

By asking herself and others how things might be different in the existing format, she became the catalyst for change. The group was finally able to become a collaborative planning group for change. "Stars don't ask, they tell," said Sarah, and went on to note that by her actions, Kathleen gave permission to others to act differently; as an instance of circular response, the group did begin behaving differently. They integrated Kathleen's perspective with their own, creating a new way of functioning for the group. In relating this story she said, "It's fascinating to see that even people who have long histories in these behaviors, when someone else raises the issue, they are willing and actually want to change." This creative possibility exists for all as we integrate the knowledge and experience of both strands of the double helix into the whole.

Out of Women's Experience:
School Leadership for Women and Men

Conceptualization of role differentiation through the metaphor of the double helix reveals a missing body of knowledge and experience about school leadership derived from the lives below the fault. Consideration of Follett's theoretical perspective on the functioning of organizations reveals that the double helix is not simply two strands linked together but a functional whole different from either of its two parts. As we come to understand the feminine strand of the helix at the same level of detail with which we understand the masculine strand, creative experience through integration of both strands will move this whole a-making ahead. We turn now to the description of the feminist attributes of leadership, the missing strand.

Note

1. See, for example, Bennis, 1984, 1990; Deal, 1982; Drucker, 1954, 1990; Mintzberg, 1989; Schein, 1985; Senge, 1990; and Sergiovanni, 1984, who are representative authors in the leadership literature of the 20th century.

3

Feminist Attributes of Leadership

The double helix we propose is composed of two interlocking strands. One of those strands symbolizes the contribution to leadership grounded in men's experience, the experience described in great detail in a broad and deep literature ranging from Machiavelli's *The Prince*, written in 1513, to Senge's *The Fifth Discipline*, published in 1990. For reasons we explore in Chapter 6, a comparable wealth of detail about the feminist strand of the double helix does not exist. In this chapter, we give an initial but far from complete description of the feminist attributes.

"Merleau-Ponty has reminded us that it is in a world already spoken that we speak" (Pagano, 1990, p. vii). In naming the feminist attributes, we use words in a world already spoken, but to these words, we have given definitions that speak to our own knowledge and practice of relational leadership. For example, to understand how courage is a feminist attribute, one must set loose, as much as possible, old connotations of that word and read actively, open to new nuances of meaning arising from women's experience of leadership.

The Five Attributes:
Collaboration, Caring, Courage, Intuition, Vision

The first attribute we have named is *collaboration:* We define collaboration as the ability to work in a group, eliciting and offering
support to each other member, creating a synergistic environment for
everyone. "Cooperativeness as women have practiced it through the
ages is one of women's hidden sources of power" (Lenz & Myerhoff,
1985, p. 10). This quality comes up over and over as we listen to
stories women tell of their experiences. Their behavior is inclusive.
They reach out to other people; they ask for help when they need it;
they gather people in, collaborating to get the job done. A significant
by-product that often results from this approach is the development
of new leadership and greater self-esteem for those empowered
through shared ownership.

Inclusiveness and shared ownership are evident in the image of
the web that Helgesen (1990) weaves when she describes the behaviors of the business and industry leaders she interviewed. The
women talked about themselves as being in the center of things and
reaching out, rather than at the top reaching down. Their language
was an expression of what they unconsciously considered desirable
and good. Their sense of self was inseparable from their sense of
connectedness to others, binding them "as if by invisible strands or
threads." This image of an interrelated structure constructed of radi-
als and orbs built around a strong central structure made Helgesen
think of a spider's web, "that delicate tracery, compounded of the
need for survival and the impulse of art, whose purpose is to draw
other creatures to it" (pp. 44-45).

Connectedness is inherent in the school community. From their
first experience as student teachers until their last days in the classroom, the language of teachers reflects their sense of being connected: They refer to their students as "my kids" or "my students."
Our experience in schools tells us that the most successful educational leaders maintain this connectedness to students and to their
staffs when they move into administering. They create collaborative
experiences for their staffs and for the students in their care. This is
reflected in Sarah's comment, "I think something women do is to give
permission to other people to behave differently." By modeling the

feminist attributes, we give people permission to act collaboratively and in a caring manner.

The second attribute, *caring,* we define as the development of an affinity for the world and the people in it, translating moral commitment to action on behalf of others. Gilligan (1982) and Belenky, Clinchy, Goldberger, and Tarule (1986) identify the themes of care and connection as central to women's psychological development and learning. And Nel Noddings (1984) tells us that "caring involves stepping out of one's personal frame of reference into the other's" (p. 24). This notion of care is very like our own. We understand care to be the essence of education; education is a project undertaken on behalf of others.

Beck (1992) identified two goals of care: promoting human development and responding to needs that are realized within interdependent relationships occurring in communities. She understands the activities of care to be receiving the other's perspective, responding to the awareness that comes from this perspective, and remaining in caring relationships over time. This description of care articulates our experience of it. We know that care directs us to the needs of students and colleagues, leads us to respond in ways that nurture their growth, and requires us to remain connected to them over long periods.

Relational leadership reflects care and concern for colleagues, male and female, and is central to our conduct of our schools. Summing up some of our thoughts on this subject, Sarah said,

> [An essential] piece of all of this is the development of relationships, and the relationships define the conditions. . . . What we've been talking about, helping others, doing unto others; it all had to do with interactions and how we can look at people, helping people develop relationships and support them and give them the environment they need to go forward . . . [establishing] trust relationships that are built on the values of caring, support, those kinds of things.

Care for children undergirds almost all our actions as leaders. Nancy was once confronted with the task of leading a group to devise a new policy for placing special education children. The union in her district had insisted on a weighting option by which some children would count more (or less) than others. In her role as chairperson of the group and in a very unobtrusive way, Nancy deflected the union's insistence on this option, although in relating the story she said, "Somewhere along the line I made it clear that there was no way in hell this was going to happen."

Clearly, Nancy was trying to come to a collaborative decision that would not violate her own value system but would allow all voices to be heard. She began the meetings by asking everyone to articulate their beliefs about children. Once the beliefs were on the table, the weighting option was unacceptable to everyone, and the group was eventually able to come up with a procedure beneficial to children and acceptable to everyone: board, administration, the teachers, and the union.

After listening to Nancy's story, Sarah noted that the uncaring attitude toward children manifested in the union's press for a weighting option simply became untenable in the context of articulated beliefs about the value of children. Arthur W. Frank, in his meditations on the care he had received through two serious illnesses, wrote the following:

> Caring has nothing to do with categories. It shows that person her life is valued because it recognizes what makes her experience particular. Care is inseparable from understanding, and like understanding, it must be symmetrical. Listening to another we hear ourselves as well. (Moyers, 1993, p. 318)

This is the essence of the care reflected in Nancy's insistence that the members of her committee articulate their beliefs about children, which forced them to listen to other voices and in so doing, to hear themselves as well. Categorizing the children became an unacceptable way to place these special children.

Relational leaders understand that the exercise of care entails the act of receiving as well as giving. Kathleen relates several incidents when she was the recipient of this care. When she was a teacher, she resisted returning to graduate school despite urging from colleagues and friends, until one day the principal of her school made an appointment with the dean of the graduate school so that she could enroll. The principal made it difficult for her to back out of the appointment when he told her, "You won't embarrass me by not showing up." He was the first of many male mentors from whom Kathleen has received care throughout her career. Her move to her current position was motivated by an unarticulated sense of dissatisfaction in her previous position, which she was able to sort through with the caring help and support of a professional friend. Through conversations with him, she was able to identify the fundamental mismatch between her values and those of the community in which she was working. This mismatch nagged at her so persistently that her move to a different community became essential to her own well-being.

"Care returns to those who give it," Kathleen remarked, going on to describe an incident that illustrates this. She has always given a holiday party for administrators in her district and for the first several years, with her husband's help, she did all of the planning and preparation. Recently, other administrators have insisted on bringing food, telling her, "You don't have to do it all. We'll help." This prompted Jan to note that Kathleen has given others, men and women, permission to care for one another, confirming Sarah's earlier statement that "something women do is to give permission to other people to behave differently." That reminded us of the transforming effect Kathleen has had on the superintendents' group in her area; the "star system," which meant competition for a hearing, has changed to collaborative behavior, where ideas join together synergistically. "Aha," said Jan, "you are creating all sorts of new possibilities for everyone, and they are popping out all over the place." That led Nancy to observe that groups of which she has been a member change fundamentally when the number of women reaches a critical proportion; competitive behavior recedes in a caring environment, and collaboration becomes possible.

Beck (1992) said, "I place caring at the top of the values hierarchy. I propose that a number of ethics have a place in educational leadership, but each needs to be informed and guided by caring" (p. 488). We agree. Care is the amniotic fluid in which all activities must be immersed.

The third attribute is *courage*, which we define as the capacity to move ahead into the unknown, testing new ideas in the world of practice. In a recent discussion with our colleagues, we discussed what the quality of courage means to us. We agreed that it involves risk taking. Nancy talked about the courage a general must have as he leads his troops into battle. Jan mentioned the kind of courage a mother displays in defending her child, and Susan spoke of the wife caring for and encouraging her husband through the last stages of cancer. We moved from talking about these kinds of courage to the kinds of courage we have had to find in dealing with situations arising in our careers. Jan said courage is the quality of leaving oneself vulnerable, of "hanging in" with a difficult situation and seeing it through. She went on to say that women take risks for the good of the group or the individual. Susan further articulated this when she said,

> When women are courageous, they aren't saying, "Here, look at me—look at what I'm doing"; instead they exercise courage in support of the organization. They take the high road and encourage everyone in the organization to achieve the high road with them. Their kind of leadership doesn't call attention to the leader; it calls attention to everybody because it's participatory and collaborative.

The people at the top of the pyramid have almost always been males. Women embarking on careers traditionally associated with men have had to take risks, confront the possibility of failure, of not fitting the mold, of enduring the many problems of being female in a male-based environment. In one of our earlier discussions, Nancy observed that

> Men know how to compete with each other. . . . There's a set of rules established in that particular arena and when a competent female comes along, they're terrified [and] in some ways it gives us more opportunity to do some things the men aren't able to do.

Kristen emphasized that there is a separation of the private and public spheres; the public sphere is a male sphere, structured by male rules that we had to figure out how to play. Kathleen made the point that we had to play by the rules to get into the group to begin with, and, she said,

That is the dilemma. How do you get into the group so you can be an effective member of that group and make change? And what attributes does one have to display in order to gain acceptance and to change those accepted behaviors?

We find Kathleen's remarks reflected in Spender (1987), who said that because of the patriarchal structure that exists, women

> are damned if we go along with it, and damned if we do not. . . . If we indicate that we have learnt the rules for making sense of the world in our patriarchal society and have become "full" members of our community, then we demonstrate that we accept the dominant view of the world, we accept the authenticity of male experience, we accept our "inferiority." (p. 2)

It has been our experience that to a point, Spender is correct, but we and many of our female colleagues accepted the authenticity of the male experience only until we began to listen to our own inner gyroscope. Embedded in the attribute of feminist care is the notion of equality; inferiority is an unacceptable condition. Our actions are driven by care, for ourselves and others. We cannot express this more effectively than does Noddings (1984), who advocates behavior that is not rule bound. This way of behaving is beautifully expressed in the writing of Ralph Waldo Emerson, which Noddings uses to explain her notion of caring behavior in behalf of others. Emerson advocated

> the sort of behavior that is conditioned not by a host of narrow and rigidly defined principles but by a broad and loosely defined ethic that molds itself in situations and has a proper regard for human affections, weaknesses, and anxieties. . . . It recognizes and calls forth human judgment across a wide range of fact and feeling, and it allows for situations and conditions in which judgment (in the impersonal, logical sense) may properly be put aside in favor of faith and commitment. (p. 25)

Kristen voiced what seemed to be a generally true course of action for each of us as we entered what had 20 years earlier essentially been a male-dominated sphere.

I know I personally experimented with the rules. First of all, I had to figure out what the rules were in that sphere, and I experimented a little bit with conforming to them, but that was short-lived. The rules I valued in my private life were also the way I have tried to behave as a leader, and any success I've had rests in being a person of integrity and having a sense of what is right or wrong. The central value is an inclusive rather than an exclusive one that devalues competition and enhances the value of collaboration and because those aren't operating in the public sphere—confrontation, competition in sports or war or whatever metaphor we want to use, when one individual enters that arena and brings a different set of rules with her, it's transformational.

We agreed that it took courage to enter such an alien world, struggle to decipher and apply a different set of rules, and then go on to change them when it became apparent that they conflicted with our core values as women. However, when the obstacles to making change are immovable and/or in conflict with our values, we have tended to move on, with or without another job in hand. This is another kind of courage, moving ahead into the unknown in a different way. Carla, referring to her departure from a job she loved in many respects, said, "I couldn't stay there anymore and continue to be healthy. That battle couldn't be won. . . . I don't know that it felt so courageous in the beginning; it felt like something I wanted to win, but couldn't."

Kathleen, a superintendent who had recently changed districts, said,

In my last job I could have stayed there forever . . . good system, well-paid, but not a satisfier. The value system I just found so appalling to my own personal core of values that [in searching for a new position], I was extremely careful as to the kind of district I would look at. The fit of the community had to be closer to my personal beliefs.

If she had stayed, she would have retained all the accoutrements of the upper ranges of the pyramid; money, prestige, power in that community.

This quality of courage is also apparent in the reflections of Bethene LeMahieu, an assistant superintendent and NECEL member, who writes about a time when she was unemployed and searching for a new position.

> I sorted things out and established criteria by which to choose the situation in which I would work next; certainties emerged. These certainties included meaningful work with people so diverse that together we could do anything, and loving what I would be doing . . . for that is how I choose to "kneel and touch the earth."

Bethene was not willing to accept just any position, even though she remained unemployed for many months. She was unwilling to compromise her values. She was determined that her new position must be in

> a setting in which there was caring, where the capacities for concern and connection were prized and nurtured, and where work was done collaboratively. . . . I was looking for leadership that enjoyed envisioning how things might be, would model or risk doing things differently, and looked upon new and unusual ideas as signs of life and growth. (LeMahieu, 1990, p. 17)

Later, she wrote, "The more courage we have to be ourselves, the more chance we have of living in communities that fit us" (LeMahieu, 1993, p. 5).[1]

This intuitive sense of self gave each of these women the courage to move on to places that were compatible with their own firmly held beliefs. This leads us to the fourth attribute, *intuition*, which we define as the ability to give equal weight to experience and abstraction, mind and heart. Intuition is a word that we as women, particularly professional women, have hesitated to use because for so long it was a "female thing," something magical usually attributed to women, as in "a woman's intuition," and therefore given little credibility. There's nothing magical about intuition. It is a natural mental ability, strongly associated with experience. In their extensive discussion of intuition, Noddings and Shore (1984) note that they accepted Kant's concept of intuition, "that capacity of mind that reaches objects directly. . . . [where] understanding is properly associated with intuition itself, and intuition provides both will and reason with representations" (p. 66).

Our experience mirrors this description of intuition. By listening to our hearts, as we call it, we come into contact with many things that are important but that our reason, unaided by intuition, would miss initially. These may be first articulations of decisions or creative resolutions of difficult problems. The representation of the decision or the solution then becomes the material on which our reason goes to work, hammering out the detail, rendering the intuition intelligible to others, building support for its validity. This is not to say that the process does not also work in reverse, with the analysis of reason providing food for intuition. It is to say, however, that intuition as the initiator is the capacity of mind and heart that is integral to a relational approach to leadership.

We have noticed that as we build on our experiences, we place greater trust in our intuition. In a discussion of the connection between familiarity and intuition, Noddings and Shore (1984) further noted that the people who are most knowledgeable in an area are those who have the most frequent and reliable intuitions. This is the case where intuition follows. This may explain why female teachers spend longer periods of time in the classroom than do their male colleagues before moving into administrative positions. Through long and deep experience in the classroom, they may intuitively know when to expand their influence into a larger sphere. Kristen remembers a time early in her career (after 5 or 6 years in the classroom), when her thoughts turned "sharply to the right," and she knew she could not remain in the classroom for the next 30 years of her life. She knew that she must move on to do something stimulating and exciting, making her choices based on her intrinsic set of values. This is an example of intuition following experience. Kristen's intuition told her it was time to move on.

However, we also have had intuitions that were not directly or obviously related to objective knowledge. We agree with Noddings and Shore (1984), who say that "intuition may operate effectively through metaphorical domains" (p. 65). This is often the case in which intuition leads.

The conceptualization of the double helix underlying this book is a cogent example of intuition leading through operation in the metaphorical domain. So is the exquisite moment in the Conversers Conference (see Chapter 5), when we realized each of us was physically touching her heart, symbolizing the deeply held beliefs that guide each of us in our practice as school leaders. Once we recognize the lead of intuition, the work of communicating its message to others begins. Sarah said,

> I think an important piece for women leaders is to articulate what they do and what they feel, what they believe, and maybe some of that comes from articulating our intuition. We may know things at a gut level, [but] unless we're articulating them, they are not going to get passed on.

As our understanding of relational leadership has matured, we have become more explicit about honoring intuition as Kathleen did throughout a complex high school reorganization project.

Faced with the task of a reorganization of the central office and the high school, Kathleen organized a study group to formulate a plan. The people involved in the study group, as well as others in the community, questioned her sharply about her plan for the high school reorganization. She responded that she did not have a plan for the reorganization, and that if she did, there would be no need for the study group. Rather she genuinely expected to learn from the work of the study group. She cited this continuous pressure on her to produce a plan single-handedly as an example of how others who have a different conception of leadership, in which the leader is the answer person sitting atop the pyramid all-knowing and all-wise, will try to force you to behave as they conceive you should. Only because of her fundamental belief in the value of collaboration was she able to resist being pressured to act without the benefit of the wisdom and experience of others. Kathleen not only resisted the pressure to act unilaterally but also explained to her constituency why she resisted, thereby educating others about her vision of leadership and helping them to redefine their own vision of leadership. Kathleen added that initially as a school leader she used to articulate only her structural sense of how a project should go, but now she goes right after the feelings, thereby honoring intuition and inviting others to do the same.

The last attribute we have named is *vision*, the ability to formulate and express original ideas, enabling others to consider options in new and different ways. A close reading of our definition of vision indicates that it is not a destination, not a product. It is not a place to which the leader guides followers, but rather a process through which the leader enables everyone to synthesize what may first appear to be disparate points of view but that, when synthesized, create a totally new and progressive position. This is Follett's creative integration. Vision, as we define it, is one of the facets of collaboration, and vice versa. Eliciting everyone's thoughts and creating a trusting environment where everyone feels free to offer his or her own points of view makes vision possible.

Here we encounter difficulties with language yet again as we enter new territory. Vision as a process is really a verb, although the word, as now understood in English, is a noun, connoting (mistakenly from our standpoint) the idea of product. Perhaps *visioning* will one day become accepted usage as *impacting* has become recently, but for now that sounds too awkward even to us who are suggesting a new meaning for the word. We solve the problem, temporarily at least, by using the term *being visionary* to mean formulating and expressing new ideas, enabling others to consider options in new and different ways. Nancy recently expressed our notion of what vision is when she said being visionary "is not to change the way things are done, but the way you want them to be. If you know what you want things to be, there may be myriad ways to get there."

The attributes of care and collaboration operate to require us to see being visionary as a process. Writing about leadership in management, Mintzberg (1989) made the point that leadership is not theater. He maintained that leaders who act the parts they do not live are destined to fall from grace: "It is integrity—a genuine feeling behind what the leader says and does—that makes leadership truly visionary . . . drama but not play acting . . . style and strategy coupled together" (p. 122). When we understand vision in this context, we are better able to understand the feelings of the women who entered administration early on and felt the uneasiness of the disjuncture between their actions and their firmly held beliefs. They were playing the part they were led to believe was required. It was only when their style met strategy, that is, when their actions became consistent with their beliefs, that they emerged as visionary leaders. Visionary leadership is trusting one's intuition. To impose a vision of our own on others would be the antithesis of care and collaboration. Rather care and collaboration, guided by intuition, make possible bringing conception of a vision to its enhanced realization. We conceive vision as dynamic, ongoing, enriched by encounters with the knowledge, beliefs, experience, and understandings of others. We are being visionary as we invite and incite others to the conversation of defining it. We're willing, even insistent that we spend time and energy developing it, knowing that the shared understanding coming from being visionary together is essential for making choices in a limited world.

We understand vision and intuition operating together when we hear in the stories of women leaders the sense of understanding the global nature of their positions as leaders. In speaking of her early classroom experiences, Kathleen says, "I was always dismayed at the narrowness in secondary schools particularly, of the isolation of the staff, and always thought there were things that could have been done—didn't know what they were back then," but she goes on to say that she had a vision in the broad sense of always being able to take in the whole and not the parts. This intuitive understanding of the whole and not the parts manifests itself in structuring a collaborative process through which a high school is redesigned, a process both visionary and courageous. Many possibilities were elicited for the reorganization, which could then be integrated in new and different ways. Through this process, Kathleen, the leader, was able to put forth her ideas as her contribution to the workings of the process, but her ideas were not privileged by virtue of her title, superintendent. To the contrary, she knew reliance on her ideas alone would lead to a plan that would be less creative than it could be if the synergistic process of being visionary were allowed to flourish. Thus she resisted pressure from others who conceive the world hierarchically to promulgate "her plan."

Reflectively, we realize we were being visionary (and courageous) when we invited our colleagues to the writers conference that evolved into the Conversers Conference we discuss in Chapter 5. We had no preconceived outcomes for the conference. Rather, we "trusted the dance," and all were rewarded. Sarah said about our conversations, "This is not just increasing my understanding; it is absolutely changing my thinking." The unfolding that took place at that 2-day conference illustrates the power of unrestricted conversation not shaped toward a predetermined end. How unlike the way bureaucracies operate. It does not surprise us that they are not creative.

Jan must frequently deal with an intractable board of education, which is unwilling, or unable, to conceive of new and different ways of managing the schools in her district. She says, "Vision is making a commitment to changing the culture. It is courageous, taking us behind the scenes [where we are] tenacious, absolutely dogged, persistent. . . . If our visions were to become the way we do things, schools would be better places."

Bureaucracies, including schools, are intended to suppress creativity, and in this they are eminently successful. Ferguson (1984), contended that bureaucracies are set up to maintain social control. She maintained, "The feminist project is to seek grounds for an alternative mode of discourse, and to articulate an alternative vision of society, that can both comprehend society, and go beyond it" (p. 6). Being visionary leaders, as we define it, is a contribution to the feminist project, presenting as it does an alternative vision for schools and the larger society.

In an essay in *Toward Reconceiving Women and Leadership* (NECEL, 1987; all quotations from p. 15), Bethene LeMahieu tells about her experience creating a school of the future, a school that was inclusive, where "teachers believed in students and confirmed them as knowers—as craftspersons, people who could do many things well." She writes that she was "propelled by inner fire—it was a time when she studied, reflected upon, practiced, and talked about developing potential in a voice marked with enthusiasm, emotion, passion, and a sense of optimism and hope." Bethene was being visionary for an entire school community, and she inspired the teachers to be visionary for students as well. The salutary effects on her spirit are manifest in her words: "Being visionary is deeply satisfying."

Firmly Held Beliefs

Our most recent conversation about the feminist attributes of leadership led us to uncover a foundation in which they are embedded. Nancy observed that a leader is a person who operates by a strong belief or value system. This observation lies at the heart of our notion of relational leadership: We operate from a foundation of firmly held beliefs.

"Feminist theory is at its best when it reflects the lived experiences of women, when it bridges the gap between mind and body, reason and emotion, thinking and feeling" (Jagger, 1983, p. x). As we tell our stories, in whatever forum, we bridge the gaps. During the Conversers Conference, from which many of the stories in this book are taken, we laughed and kidded each other about touching our hearts as we told our stories and discussed our values; we spoke of maintaining the balance and centeredness of our lives built on the foundation of our beliefs. Jan introduced the metaphor of a gyroscope buried in our centers. Sarah called it a directive force that guides us when we are confronted with life's choices. Our gyroscopes keep us balanced and aligned. Suddenly we see that this is the belief system Kathleen knew she was operating out of from the start; the force that impelled her to confront the union representative who was browbeating the faculty into signing a petition against their principal. It is the belief system that prompted Kristen's decision to move from the classroom to a leadership position, from which she knew she could make a difference. Her decision was based on her intrinsic values. She observed that although they are definitely satisfiers, she is not motivated by the external rewards of power, money, status; however, she quickly pointed out that "If I'm paid far less than I'm worth, then I feel exploited and I draw the line there."

Sarah had begun this line of conversation, which ebbed and flowed over the 2 days we were with one another. Her earliest dream of her adult life, she recalled, was of having a life of personal satisfaction through influencing the lives of others. The exact nature of her work was less important to her. Her firmly held beliefs led her to leave high school before graduation, and without ever receiving a high school diploma, she entered herself into the baccalaureate program from which she graduated. Jan says her first goal was to have a fun and interesting life in a way that changes people's lives; once she hit her first administrative position, she knew she had found the path to keep doing that. Nancy reflects her firmly held beliefs when she convenes each Planning and Placement Team meeting with the statement, "If this were our child, what would we want?"

From these stories, our talk broadened to women's visions of the good life. At the bottom of it all, we require that our actions honor and respect the dignity and worth of each person we encounter, of whatever age, gender, race, or class. Our enactment of the feminist attributes of leadership constitutes the frame within which we guarantee to the best of our abilities that we are faithful to this firmly held belief. As we explore this concept further, our talk switches to retirement, which is real for us now, at mid-career. We anticipate it not as an ending but as another new beginning, a transition to the next stage in our fun and interesting lives. We see Jan, who at present is a school superintendent, revealed as the tap-dancing landlady she is already. Although only a few of her colleagues know, tap dancing is her recreation. The landlady part will underwrite her fun and interesting retirement; the tap-dancing part is about having fun now.

Sarah recalls Jennifer's story about being in a phone booth talking to a principal who wanted her to teach at the junior high school. Her response was, "I can come to the junior high if you want, but it won't be for long because I'm going into administration"—the words popping out of her mouth before she knew she had said them or had made the conscious decision to do so. Now we envision a transformational phone booth into which we each enter to undergo the metamorphosis needed to move to the next step. Suddenly we see each of us emerging from phone booths as tap-dancing landladies, an image that brought us gales of shared laughter. This pleasurable trip into the future is perhaps made possible by our earlier discussions of leader versus role. We do not understand ourselves to be one with our role. Rather, the role is one of the many we carry throughout our lives, some of which we pass in and out of naturally each day (wife, mother, companion, administrator, teacher), others that we leave behind as we transition into another phase of our lives.

In contrast to the humor and hopefulness of the images of ourselves as tap-dancing landladies emerging from phone booths is the sterility we have seen in those whose formal role is also their identity.

Lacking a set of firmly held beliefs guiding their growth as human beings into the next phase of their lives, they resist retirement, with its loss of identity and purpose. We conjecture that this loss may be exacerbated for men because from early childhood they are led to believe their role is their identity, therefore, when you are no longer superintendent, doctor, lawyer, who are you?

Later we embellish the idea of loss as we investigate our emerging understanding of our firmly held beliefs. Jennifer notes that although factual information can be parroted at any age, rich, intuitive knowledge forms well into adulthood because it requires life experience to grow. Kristen links this to our earlier notion that many of the men around us identify themselves through the role they occupy. It's possible from that perspective to master the factual knowledge associated with the role and the public sphere rules that define behavior for the role, and then to proceed through a career simply by going through the motions. No wonder retirement seems like such a black hole for many of our male colleagues who from earliest childhood have been taught that they are one with their role.

The converse of this situation occurs to us as equally sad and full of loss. We recognize that, with depressing frequency, we have encountered people in formal leadership roles who have put on the external features of that role and perform in complete absence of any firmly held beliefs. Such people are generally incapable of being visionary, are out of touch with their intuitions, are unable to foster collaboration, lack the strength to be courageous, and treat others in uncaring ways. Here we confront the question—are these leaders, or are they managers?

A leader conceives of a different world. She or he is a visionary who has the intellectual capacity to embrace the plausible and the implausible, who thinks globally and reaches beyond the moment, applying both divergent and convergent thinking to effect change. Intrinsically motivated by a moral code of conduct, a leader empowers others to achieve mutually agreed upon goals and, when necessary, guides others to behave in morally responsible ways.

Relational leadership embodies the totality of this definition of a leader. Relational leaders have a broad vision of the goals to be worked toward. They accept the fundamental responsibility for both the quality of the group process and for the product deriving from it. They work as part of the group, not separate from it, to define and achieve specific goals arrived at collaboratively. They have faith in the wisdom of the group, guiding its members toward achievement of their goals, while at the same time recognizing and celebrating the achievements and contributions of each individual involved in the process. Relational leaders, by making choices aligned with our firmly held beliefs about the dignity and worth of each individual, retain agency through which we make many small, but significant impacts on the schools in which we work. This is in sharp contrast to others who let the organization define them and thus are robbed of the power to define it.

Gender is a category of experience. The feminist attributes we have named reflect feminine experience. They emerge from an ethic of care, where the dignity of each person is honored; this ethic propels them into action on behalf of others. Articulating these attributes and naming them has brought them into consciousness. "In beginning to find out how and what to speak," wrote Smith (1987), "we had to begin from nowhere, not knowing what it was we would have to say and what it was we would need to know how to speak" (p. 58).

Kathleen summarized the impact of our discoveries by saying she has adopted a phrase from the program "Reading Recovery." The phrase "wandering around the known" is used by elementary teachers when they are wandering around what is known by the child and trying to link it up with a set of their experiences so their growth is revealed. That is what our journey has been, wandering around the known. When we began, we didn't know. Now we know that our feminine experiences are inextricably linked to our behaviors as relational leaders.

In the next chapter, we will examine the experiences of several of us, seeing how interpretation using the lens of the feminist attributes brings clarity and coherence to our actions. We look retrospectively at early projects undertaken in ignorance of the feminist attributes of leadership and at projects undertaken consciously with the attributes explicitly in mind. In all cases, we find that interpretations using the attributes bring meaning to actions and point the way.

Note

1. These quotations are published by permission of the author.

4

Relational Leadership at Work

Examining one's work from the standpoint of women's experience (see Smith, 1987), as articulated through the feminist attributes, locates past points of resistance, is a present act of resistance, and can be the platform for future, more explicit acts of resistance. Such analysis by either women or men can bring each of us up against the disjuncture between our experience and the structure within which we work and prepare us to work for change. We have chosen to examine and analyze our work through the stories that arise from our experiences. "Stories can help us understand by making the abstract concrete and accessible" (Witherell & Noddings, 1991).

We need to share our stories with each other and to retell the stories we have heard about others. By doing so, we contribute to the work of redefining leadership, and we gain confidence in the explanatory power of the feminist attributes. In this chapter we relate stories told retrospectively by two female administrators about their educational practices, one from the perspective of the novice, the other the perspective of an experienced administrator. Their experiences reflect the feminist attributes of care, collaboration, vision, intuition, and courage.

The first stories are told by Susan Villani (1990), an elementary principal who is a past president of NECEL. Her retrospective view of the earliest days of her administrative career illustrates how the feminist attributes can bring clarity and coherence to a narrative that at first seems disjointed, without connecting themes. We offer it as an example to others who might be inspired to reflect retrospectively about their own work.

Susan Villani:
A Principal Defined

As I look back, I smile at memories of my first efforts to express the attributes of courage, caring, collaboration, vision, and intuition. We had not named those attributes then, but as I examine my career in retrospect, I see that they guided my first steps as a school principal faced with disbelief and resistance from those all around me who could not assimilate the fact of a woman principal. It was a difficult beginning for us all, but by embodying the feminist attributes in my leadership, even unknowingly, I was wiser than I knew.

As I began my first principalship (ironically in a school named "Hazard"), I was very eager to show everyone that I was the right choice for the job. I was 26, the youngest adult on the school staff, moving directly from a first-grade teaching position to the principalship of this grade 5 and 6 school, and I was nervous. Early that first morning, I met the man who had been the school principal until he had transferred to another school in the same town. He offered to help me place the fifth graders entering my school from the fourth grades in two of the elementary schools in town. He walked over to the telephone that had once been his and dialed the other principal. "Hello, John, this is Al. I'm in the new little girl's office." I barely heard the rest of his sentence, being so stunned by the comment he had made without the slightest idea of the impact it would have on me.

As we waited for John to arrive, Al reflected on his years as principal. He was a tall, muscular man, a former athlete who struck an imposing stance. "Some of the kids here are very tough," he told me. "I used to play a little basketball with them, one on one, you know. And somehow after we played they got the message and they would straighten out." He looked me over, noting my petite height and frame, and then added, almost with a note of concern, "I don't know what you're going to do." I thought about his words and wondered if I should immediately go out and register for a karate class. Instead, I intuitively knew that my only hope would be to use another strategy. I knew I couldn't do it his way. I didn't know what my way would be, but I had to find a way that used the strengths I knew I had.

I walked into what was to be my office and encountered a barricade. The former principal had arranged a large, gray metal desk and two gray filing cabinets in a row, facing the entrance to the office. I knew I couldn't work in such an environment and set about to tear it down and build one that was right for us—the children, staff, parents, and me. I wanted an office that was welcoming, warm, and would be comfortable for myself and anyone who joined me.

In the spirit of finding a way to make my office reflect my style, I set about to find some wooden furniture, scouring the attics of many of the schools and the administration building. People were confused by my unwillingness to accept their generous offers to order some new metal office furniture. Eventually, I pieced together just what I wanted. I placed a refinished oak desk at a diagonal to the doorway, with a chair to the side of the desk; peering over my desk was not the way I wanted to begin conversations. Then I bought a braided rug on which I put oak chairs with braided chair pads in an oval configuration. An oak filing cabinet and smaller pieces of furniture met the remaining utilitarian needs. Because I could not use the fluorescent lights, I completed my office renovations with several floor lamps. I intended to keep my door open, but I placed a tapestry over the glass insert for the times requiring privacy when the door could be firmly closed. Finally, I hung student artwork to create a special aesthetic feeling in my new surroundings. I was beginning to tell the community who I was and how I envisioned connectedness among the members of our school community.

The setting of my office was only the beginning of many ways that I was trying to communicate that the principal of Hazard School not only was strong enough to meet the challenges but was a gentle and warm person as well. Despite these efforts, I was continually amazed at how strongly my staff and others clung to their old expectations of the principal. During my first year, I found that some staff were continually dissatisfied with things that I was doing, yet I had initial difficulties pinpointing exactly why they were dissatisfied. One day when I pushed one staff member to tell me, she blurted out, "When Al was here, it was different. He was like a father to us." I was stung by her words. My head throbbed as I doubted that I would ever be able to be the principal they said they wanted. I could never be a father for whom some longed, and I knew I didn't want to be a mother to them either.

In the minds of some people, the image of a principal is firmly rooted in stereotypes of age and gender. For example, occasionally visitors would encounter me in the front office with the school secretary, a woman older than myself, and the teacher's aide, a man approximately my age. In their search for the principal, the visitor would first look at the teacher's aide and ask if he was the principal. When he indicated that he was not, the visitor would turn next to the secretary. Upon learning that she too was not the principal, they would at last look at me and ask, "Where is the principal?" These incidents added to my concerns about whether I would ever be widely regarded as the rightful inhabitant of my position.

Although I tried to reassure myself by focusing on the inappropriateness of everyone's expectations, my pain in not meeting their needs and my own was excruciating. I often felt overwhelmed with the sense that my efforts to create a sense of community among such diverse and often antagonistic members of the staff were futile. It was clear that to many, my presence was more of an upset than a unifying catalyst. I was not the principal anyone expected—not male, not middle-aged, and not physically imposing. Often I felt little hope that a real principal, in anyone's eyes but mine, could be female, young, and petite. Could I ever be seen as worthy, or was I always to remain an aberration, maybe even a fraud, in the estimation of others?

Although the landscape seemed bleak almost everywhere I looked, I did find a few people in the community with whom I shared a vision about schools and education. We were mutually elated to find kindred spirits and gravitated toward each other. Together we undertook three major initiatives at the Hazard School that helped define me as a principal in the eyes of myself and others and that empowered others to contribute meaningfully to our school and community. In retrospect I understand that through collaboration, we brought to life a shared vision, following our intuitions and acting courageously to demonstrate care for the children and adults in the school and community. In so doing, my negative identity as "not Al" gradually melted away. I became Susan, a principal characterized by the practice of what we have now named the feminist attributes of leadership.

CELEBS: A Way to Bring
Pieces of the Community Together

My first story begins with Roberta Sherman, a resource teacher at Hazard School. Roberta conceived the program Career Exploration Linking Essential Basic Skills (CELEBS) out of her growing concern that students were not motivated to learn basic skills because they did not understand the need for them. Her idea was to involve people from the community (many of them parents and neighbors of our students) in a dialogue with our students about the basic skills needed in the performance of a variety of jobs. Bringing community people into the school to talk about their jobs, Roberta felt, would motivate students who aspired to one of these jobs to take more seriously their need to acquire the basic skills of reading, writing, and computing.

Once I had the sense of what this program might do for our students, I shared our vision with Anne Christner, one of our parents and a faculty member at the state university located nearby. She enthusiastically joined us in planning the program, and collaboration with her added two additional perspectives to our discussions. As a parent she underscored my own intuition about the power of including parents and other adult members of the community, and through her academic connections, she linked us to invaluable sources of information and expertise.

Our initial outreach to members of the community through the CELEBS program was greeted with great enthusiasm. We had more offers than we could initially use from people in many different occupations and age groups. Our initial group included a lobsterer, an

advertising consultant, an architect, a social worker, a nursing administrator, and a consumer educator.

The children were fascinated when our CELEBS described their
work. The program was a great success with the students and with
the adults who became involved in it. The feminist attributes came
alive, not only through the collaborative leadership of Roberta, Anne,
and myself, but also through the CELEBS themselves. They expressed care by taking time to talk about their work and themselves
with the youngsters. They were part of the collaborative effort to
respond to the needs of children. They were courageous to come and
face a group of students in a classroom, something they initially
found very threatening. Yet they did it because they shared our vision
of preparing youngsters through the development of basic skills and
their relationship to the world of work.

I believe that through my leadership in CELEBS, the staff learned
about my vision for quality education and about my courage to try
new things. They also learned that I would work very hard for things
I believed in for the school community. I now realize one of my initial
strengths in my first principalship was the feminist attribute of collaboration. Through collaboration with Roberta and Anne, listening
to our minds and our hearts, we collectively created a vision that was
developed with a depth and fullness that responded to the needs of
the school and community in ways that I alone could not have done.
The cumulative effect of our combined talents surpassed any we
would have had as individuals. This is the essence of leadership as
we are redefining it. Moreover, CELEBS enabled many people to see
me as a successful leader for the first time, giving me hope that my
status as "not Al" would be permanently replaced by a view of me
as Susan, Hazard School Principal.

Further Career Exploration:
One Initiative Spawns Another

Encouraged by the gradual endorsement of CELEBS by the staff
and urged on by our memories of the lively and significant discussions among CELEBS and our students, Anne and I found we shared
a mutual vision of children thinking about careers based on their individual talents, skills, and needs and unrestrained by sex role stereo-

typing in their career selection and goal setting. We cared about each individual and wanted each to be empowered to act in her or his best interest and in ways that would encourage meaningful contribution to the larger group. Because we knew that parents often have the greatest impact on their children's aspirations, we decided that any efforts to influence children to expand their thinking would require equal efforts with their parents so that the new awareness would not die from lack of validation. So our vision grew to include adults as well as children and out of this came the two career programs briefly described here.

The Career Exploration Program

Anne, who was dedicated to providing a model of male and female teams working together toward a common goal, enlisted a male colleague from the university to work with her. Together they developed a minicourse about work that they presented as a team to different classes. They designed a curriculum based on work, money, and the economy. The students not only learned the curriculum of the course but also learned a great deal about men and women working in equal partnership to achieve a common goal.

Simultaneous with the course Anne and her partner created, I developed a course about careers and sex-role stereotyping, which I piloted with a fifth-grade class. I found the students eager to discuss their feelings about the world in which they found themselves. I was deeply touched by their candor, yet troubled by their experience of the world in 1981. Although some may think, "You've come a long way, baby," their responses made it clear that we had a long way to go. However, in addition to my reactions to what the students said, I had very powerful feelings about the fact that we were engaged in such a meaningful process of sharing our core beliefs. The elation I felt from my experience with the students highlighted my sorrow in the lack of connection I felt with some of the staff.

The Career Cornucopia Program

Asking children to look at stereotypes takes courage. Risking conflict with family or societal values requires a firm conviction that the possible outcome is worth the effort and discomfort some may feel. We knew that parental endorsement would be a critical factor in the ability (or willingness) of some students to assimilate the expanded awareness about career we would be teaching. We felt that the stakes were high, and we were ready to make the investment. Our caring for the children and the future they would help create fueled our vision; our success with CELEBS fueled our energies for creating the Career Exploration and Cornucopia Programs.

Involving parents, I was convinced, was crucial to making new ideas about careers come alive for students. I also kept thinking about how fascinated all of the adults were when we were meeting with the CELEBS and coaching them about how to share their careers with students. We kept getting sidetracked from our original goal because we had so many questions of each other. It made sense to me to have an educational event for parents at which adults could satisfy their curiosity about careers, along with our students. Through collaboration of many people, Career Cornucopia was born. It was a multimedia event in the school after the school day was over. It involved parents, students, and community in a variety of activities focused on a variety of careers and designed to interest students and adults. The magnitude and success of the undertaking exemplified what can be achieved through collaboration on a shared vision.

This experience, building on our earlier success with CELEBS, also had personal implications for my developing identity as the principal of Hazard School. Through enactment of the feminist attributes of leadership embodied in the Career Exploration and Career Cornucopia Programs, the aberrant principal, "not Al," was fading, and the authentic principal, Susan, was emerging.

The Cultural Awareness Program:
Vision, Collaboration, and Courage in Action

The third major initiative I undertook was perhaps the most powerful because of its intensity and scope. The roots for the Cultural Awareness Program lay in a conversation that I had about a year after becoming the principal of Hazard School. The conversation had made a big impression on me, and I mulled it over and over in my head. I remember it as if it were yesterday.

"How do you like being the principal of the Hazard School?"

"I like it very well," I said. "The community is so diverse—I find it very rich."

"Rich?" said another woman, sounding perplexed. "I thought that some of the kids that go to that school are poor."

This was said by an educated person who worked in a school herself. And she is not alone. Many people operate on the misconception that richness is measured by dollars, and the more the better. I believed that our students would be cheated if they did not develop an appreciation for the many gifts that people have to offer. Just as variety is the spice of life, so diversity in cultural and socioeconomic background brings a richness to the community.

By pondering the implications of this conversation over many months, I had unwittingly prepared my mind much the same as a compost pile of discarded organic materials produces rich soil. When Carol Grandin, the parent who spearheaded the idea of the Cultural Awareness Program, spoke with me, the seed she planted found a ready environment.

Carol, who is white, wanted to create a program that would address the lack of multicultural awareness in our community and present alternatives to racism. In a proposal for this program, Carol wrote,

I feel that my children have natural advantages not afforded all children. While I do not want them to feel guilty because of their birth luck, I do want them to understand how racism hurts our nation and threatens our greatness as a people. I want them to act responsibly and responsively. They are the future of our nation and they have a chance and an obligation to change what past and present generations have chosen to ignore.

Clearly this was a vision of great importance, offered by an intelligent and articulate woman of strong character. Her caring was enhanced by her readiness to do a lot of groundwork that would be necessary to create such a program. From Carol's letter and our discussions that followed, the vision became reality. We found we had the courage to share the vision with others, and as we did, the collaboration kept growing to include people who believed as we did that appreciation of differences comes from knowledge about them, and from knowledge comes understanding. From this collaboration of like-minded people, the Cultural Awareness Program was created.

As our group grew, I could feel our strength as surely as if assessing the muscles of a weight lifter. We needed to feel our power, for realizing our vision would require great strength of mind and spirit. We relied on each other's knowledge, each other's experiences, and each other's intuition as we charted our course.

We acted on our belief that appreciation and understanding of differences comes from knowledge. We decided that our cultural awareness program would focus on the histories of the African American and Native American populations because their heritages are so much a part of the county in which we live. Local citizens could tell about their roots, and we could visit important landmarks and places of continuing importance in the African American and Native American communities.

We believed this approach would benefit everyone. The students in our school and community members of these two cultures would have the opportunity to share what they already knew and learn more about their heritage. The members of the majority population would learn a great deal about African American and Native American history and culture. We hoped that our children would become aware of and confront feelings of prejudice. Prejudice is present in all of us, and through our honest exploration of attitudes, we all learned more about ourselves in the process of learning about each other. I believe that as a result of our Cultural Awareness Program, we moved a step closer to going through life enriched. In this sense, the students that went to Hazard School were far from poor; indeed they became richer than ever.

The Cultural Awareness Program was a 4-year endeavor. It grew from a conversation between a parent, Carol, and myself, a school administrator, into a powerful series of experiences for children and adults that had a cumulative benefit. It was like making bread. The ingredients were healthy. The bakers knew that the climate of the school and community were as essential for a satisfying outcome as is the necessity for the flour and yeast to be the correct temperature. It took many hands to knead the bread, to work with it until it felt right. It took time, patience, and love. And when it was ready, it was a feast for the hungry. In our case, the hungry were the people who had experienced racism and were hungry for respect and equity. Other people were hungry to be part of a solution to racism. And the children were hungry, perhaps unconsciously at first, to know themselves and their classmates more completely. It was a very nourishing meal.

The collaboration that grew from the initial vision that Carol shared with me was one of the most powerful experiences of my life. It took courage on the part of many people to carry it out. Although many supported the program—leaders from the university, who provided their expertise; the teachers at Hazard School, who demonstrated their caring and creativity in their classrooms; and the African American and Native American leaders, who gave the program credibility through their experiences and backgrounds—not everyone supported it. Significant racial intolerance and hatred were revealed in letters to the editor of the newspaper. Others thought it was a bad idea, predicting racial tension, or even more discouraging, they didn't think the issues were worth the effort.

In retelling the story of our three initiatives at Hazard School, I am still moved by the power of our collaboration in sharing our visions with the community. And I am struck by the depth of courage of the leaders of these initiatives. I don't believe that we thought much about our courage as we were doing what we had a passion to do. Yet in retrospect, initiating these innovations took courage and a great deal of inner strength as we set out to bring to reality our vision for our children.

I am most thankful to the many colleagues I was blessed to have during this time. They helped me in my journey in transforming my identity as the principal who was "not Al" to my authentic identity as the principal, Susan, one of many women and men who employ the feminist attributes of leadership on behalf of our schools and communities. I hope the telling of these stories empowers others to continue or initiate similar journeys where each in her or his particular way, and in large and small ways, brings the practice of feminist attributes of leadership to his or her work as a school leader.

✧ ✧ ✧

Susan's story illustrates how interpretation of actions taken in ignorance of leadership using the five attributes brings coherence and clarity to those actions. Rather than being the idiosyncratic decisions of one woman, they become solid examples of how implementation of the feminist attributes enrich school life for the entire community. Susan's story inspires ideas in others, both women and men, about ways in which they too can employ the feminist attributes to benefit their schools. In the next section, we describe smaller examples of how several of us, made impatient by our new knowledge, spoke out more forcefully about change.

Mentoring and Modeling the Attributes

Maybe because we're older, maybe because we're wiser, probably a little of both, we find ourselves in more of a hurry. We are not satisfied with having identified and named the feminist attributes, nor with having used them to bring clarity and coherence to our own career paths. We are eager to have others learn them as well. Jan, after witnessing a faculty meeting in which the teachers complained bitterly about how parents contributed to an unsafe dismissal of children, said forcefully and directly, "The parents are not our enemy. You have to get them in here so you and they can work together to ensure the safety of the children as school dismisses." A few years ago, she would have been reluctant to communicate her beliefs quite so directly. As Kathleen says, "Time is too short to tolerate nonsense."

Through experience we now have the confidence to assert our firmly held beliefs. In many small ways, we work daily to teach others the feminist attributes. Of course, we do it naturally and almost unconsciously through the example of our own actions and words, but we also do it purposefully and explicitly. Many of us, informally and formally through our professional organizations, have mentored both women and men aspiring to or just entering administrative and other leadership positions. As a high school administrator, Gwen found it deeply satisfying to serve as mentor to several aspiring administrators, women and men, through an administrative internship program sponsored by the school district in which she worked and another sponsored by the Women and Minorities program of the

Leadership in Educational Administration Development Center (LEAD), a collaborative effort of the Center, the Connecticut State Department of Education, and other education agencies in the state. In a letter to Gwen, referring to the results of the formal evaluation of the project by the mentors and "mentees," Kathy Rockwood (personal communication, September 20, 1988), director of the project, wrote, "The quality and impact of these relationships were overwhelmingly positive," an observation confirmed over time. These mentees have expressed their feelings that the support of their mentors and the experience they gained helped them in obtaining their first administrative positions and gave them increased confidence in meeting the challenges of these positions. In our present academic positions as educators and trainers of new teachers, we, the authors, model through our actions and words the feminist attributes that we hope our students will integrate into their ways of teaching and leading.

In her latest superintendency, Kathleen has hired three new principals, all women, in her district. Understanding that they would need the courage born of association with other women who experience the jobs as they do and delighted that for the first time in her career, there were enough women to form a functioning group, she encouraged the administrators to enroll in continuing education classes together. As Kathleen told her story, we laughed at the brilliance of their choice of eucalyptus wreath making. Although the invitation to join them was extended to the male administrators, none accepted, as Kathleen intended. She secured a safe, female-based environment in which she could teach her new women colleagues, surrounded by the welcoming fragrance of eucalyptus and enmeshed in the satisfying handiwork of making wreaths. If Kathleen were a man, she would likewise make use of her gender to organize a trip to a New York Rangers game or a fishing expedition. Same-sex activity has an educational role, as participants can share common experience rooted in gender as a category of experience. This is not to say that Kathleen does not also attend to the education of her male colleagues. Among other experiences, she has arranged an early-morning study group of men and women who come to discuss readings from books she has given them as gifts. She tells them, "The book is a gift, the discussion is your choice."

NECEL has sponsored two wilderness trips for women only. The three days of backpacking and rope climbing were led by women, and all problems they encountered in the woods were solved by the women themselves. Forced to rely on their own physical strength, probably for the first time, the women participants found that they were strong in unexpected and liberating ways. The groups continued to meet for the year following their trip, analyzing their experience within the context of shared readings and conversation and exploring its ramifications for their work as school leaders. Each of these women is called upon daily to make hard decisions that affect the lives of many, children and adults alike. The wilderness experience confirmed and enhanced their self-confidence and their faith in their ability to withstand physically and emotionally the difficult, sometimes dangerous, situations they are confronted with in their professional positions.

Each of these actions, taken in isolation, may seem too insignificant to effect real change. However, multiplied many times over and practiced over time, such actions form a critical mass that can permanently change the culture of our presently bureaucratically structured school systems. Just as Susan's story suggests how large projects organized around the feminist attributes benefit schools, so too these vignettes should suggest the summative power of many small acts, conversations, and examples to enrich schools using the five attributes.

We find that some of the change we desire comes about through the actions we take each day as we routinely go about our business. At other times, we find that if we are to make a difference, we must analyze our actions, articulate a formal structure, and act consciously to bring about the desired change. Guided by her intuitive sense, Helen, in a new position as principal of a high school, realized that if she were to fulfill the mission of the school through a vision shared by all members of that school, the bureaucratic structure had to be changed. Her prior administrative positions had been as an assistant principal and as an acting principal. In this new position, she would have an opportunity to bring about real change, and her vision was a school where people worked collaboratively toward a shared vision. When her first attempts at building a collaborative team failed, she knew she would have to take steps to gradually wean the staff away from the authoritarian methods to which the members of the school had been accustomed. Here Helen relates the experience that eventually led her to the elaboration of a method by which collaboration is modeled and taught directly.

Genesis of a Model
to Teach Collaboration

Whether through formal or informal experiences, we find that relational leaders seek out opportunities to lead by modeling and/or directly teaching the feminist attributes. Shortly after my move into higher education from a high school principalship, J. Patrick Howley (a colleague and private consultant) and I embarked on a project underwritten by the Connecticut Principals' Academy to teach teachers to collaborate. In my conceptualization of that project, we integrated an experiential framework for collaboration with a rationale for its use. The genesis for this model lay in my previous experiences as a new high school principal. Here is an understanding rooted in women's experience, accessed originally through intuition but rendered accessible to others through cognitive analysis.

Introduction to a Collaborative Teaching Model

Raised in a culture where competition is the dominant mode of interaction between people, it is not surprising that many of us do not arrive at the schoolhouse door with either the predisposition or the skills to use collaboration as the mode of interaction with one another. Also, the physical arrangement of space in schools, with each of us working in a classroom with no other adult, and the organization of schedules, which keeps us in those classrooms for most of the day, support our tendency to ignore one another as we do our work. The operating norm in most schools is that we as teachers are responsible for managing our own classrooms, relying on our own ingenuity and knowledge to solve any problems that may arise. In fact it is a mark of incompetence in many schools to ask for help from anyone, particularly the principal.

The relationship between principals and teachers is primarily hierarchical, perhaps even adversarial, where, through the formal organizational structure and 100 years of practice, the norm has been established that the principal has power and expertise that teachers lack. Thus teachers defer to principals in face-to-face contact, and principals feel the responsibility to be omniscient, making decisions and solving problems alone. In this system both groups are deprived of the benefit of consultation with the other. A further consequence of the hierarchical relationship between teachers and principals is an underground, where each forms opinions of the other but never reveals them. Neither group then receives feedback from the other, and opportunities to improve based on the observation and considered judgment of a colleague are lost.

The isolation of practice forced on teachers by circumstances of organization of space and time operates similarly to deprive them of the benefit of the wisdom of one another. Teachers rarely, if ever, discuss their actual planning and teaching. The physical isolation deprives us of the opportunity to see one another work, and thus we have little firsthand information about one another, and the norm prescribing independent work sets up the expectation that comment to one another about practice is in some sense a vote of no confidence. Change in such a system is hard to come by because no one feels that it is safe to offer concrete suggestions to a colleague.

As a high school principal, I wanted to change these norms. I had a vision of an environment where the operative norm was candid talk about managerial and instructional issues in our school and where each person felt a responsibility to contribute to the whole. Although I worked on these goals in public arenas from the very first day, my efforts to change these norms were concentrated on a small group with whom I had regular contact, in hopes that once norms changed there, together we could transfer the new norms to the wider school. So I set out to build a team including myself, the two assistant principals, and the department heads. I soon realized my efforts to break deeply rooted norms of competitive interaction among us had no chance of success unless I actually taught my colleagues quite specifically what new behaviors I expected. Thus I learned a very significant lesson that I have subsequently developed: As educational leaders who want to do things differently than they have been done, we must model and teach our colleagues new skills and nurture the growth of new attitudes. Change cannot occur without this direct support from us of new behaviors.

As a high school principal, I personally experienced mistrust and resistance among the members of the group I was trying to build into a team. As a first step toward building greater comfort and familiarity among us, one weekend I invited them all to my house for a holiday gathering. I hoped that by extending myself and opening up the personal space of my home to them, they would respond by opening up themselves also. Instead, through the grapevine I heard that my invitation had caused resentment because it required them to give up personal time for school business. The invitation had been received as a command that I had no right to issue outside the parameters of the workweek. I meant the invitation sincerely, and I was hurt when I realized that it was not received by many in the spirit in which I had extended it. I went ahead nonetheless. Most attended and brought food. The gathering itself was awkward, and I found myself thinking, "Why am I doing this?" However, the next day several other people and I had leftovers from the party for our lunches, and all of a sudden we were joking about who had made the best food. I realized then that although the journey was painful, still I was making progress by building a common base of personal experience from which we could begin to trust one another. Up to that moment, we had had little in common to joke about.

My next step in team building was to arrange an overnight retreat for the group. I chose the site of the retreat carefully for its aesthetic qualities. I wanted a sense of being far away in a serene atmosphere with good food and opportunity for some recreation. We went to a country inn with a pool and home-baked cranberry muffins. Although it was February and gloomy, we felt warm and cozy. I drove several group members myself and arranged carpools for others. I wanted the time in the intimacy of a car for conversation.

I also hired my first consultant for this retreat. I chose someone who had a fine reputation for team building, and I left the agenda to him. I became one of the group, as opposed to the leader of the group. One of the things he asked us to do was to draw a picture representing our hopes and intentions as we assumed our current role, be it department chair, assistant principal, or principal. As I listened to each person describe her or his drawing, I learned things about their aspirations, satisfactions, and frustrations that never surface in the conversation at formal meetings. As I spoke about my drawing, I was given an opportunity to voice my dreams and frustrations in a natural way. The distance usually imposed by my role as principal was not erased, but it was greatly reduced. I felt listened to and understood, feelings I did not often experience as a principal. The retreat was a turning point; although all of us did not always agree, from that point on, we did seem to break through the barrier that had led us to mistrust one another's motives and prevented us from hearing each other.

Throughout my tenure as a high school principal, I worked consistently to model and to articulate the practice of collaboration. With no model or experience on which to build my efforts, I listened to my intuition and acted as I thought best. I now realize that if collaboration is to take place, it must be built on a trusting relationship among all of those involved. Upon examining this particular experience some years later, I realized that I needed to create another process for beginning the trust-building process in schools where I would be a consultant, not the principal. In my role in higher education, a move I had made from public school administration, I had the luxury of time to examine retrospectively my work at teaching teachers to collaborate. Through that analysis, and with the assistance of a colleague, I conceptualized a model that we later implemented when working as consultants with other high schools.[1] As I describe the model, I also connect it to my own experiences as a high school principal so that its roots in real school life are apparent.

At the end of the 2-year project that I undertook with Patrick Howley in a Connecticut school district, I found I had learned much since my first attempts at teaching collaboration, guided by my intuition but at times hampered by my lack of experience. As a brand new principal, I knew that I was not comfortable working in an environment where the teachers were my adversaries. I wanted to tear down the old hierarchical pyramid and weave in its place a soft, but strong web that supported us all in our collective work of educating adolescents. I knew that I needed to lead the way because very few others in the school had a vision of how things could be different. I myself wasn't sure of the itinerary, but I kept experimenting.

Although I would not have called myself courageous at the time, as I look back on that experience, I see now that I did take risks, not all of which were painless.

I came out of my experience as a high school principal convinced that collaboration is a superior mode of interaction between principals and teachers because it taps strengths in both groups that the current hierarchical mode of interaction subverts. In my first attempts at collaborative team building, I did not understand that collaboration is built on trusting relationships, that this trust is built slowly over time and through shared experience. During the 2 years of acting in the capacity of consultant to a district, in which I sought to teach collaboration to teachers, I became consciously aware that people must be willing to change and adopt new ways of behaving. As I reflected back on the project, however, I came to realize from my own behavior that, although there may be willingness to change, new ways of behaving are not adopted quickly or easily. Going into the project, intellectually I knew that it was essential that I act in the role of outsider to the group I was teaching. Indigenous leadership within a group is essential if a team is to have a life of its own. Despite sincere attempts to divest myself as leader of the project, I never truly succeeded in doing so. In any situation such as this, there are likely to be behaviors that restrict the complete success of the project, and discouraging though these restricting behaviors are, they are also very real. As we attempt to teach behaviors to others, they will always remind us that we cannot be 100% successful. The collaborative method of interacting will not magically smooth out all interpersonal relationships, but it will lead to decisions that participants support, and it will contribute to the professional development of most. The design of the model describing my first fumbling attempts to create a collaborative team is one way to teach teachers how to collaborate. It supports the attempts of both teachers and principals to learn new behaviors through use of an outsider to bring meaning to a real school experience by supplying analytical frameworks through which the collaborative process can be understood.

In ways small and large, our stories are examples of ways some of us have taken steps to teach the feminist attributes to those around us. We can all do this. What is important is to speak, naming the attribute as we see it in action. Relational leaders must speak frequently, speak publicly, and speak encouragingly. In the next chapter, we describe the journey by which we constructed understanding of relational leadership. A two-decade relationship among us, sustained and nurtured by formal associations in NECEL, has led not only to new understanding but also to a new understanding of how to understand.

Note

1. An abridged description of this model previously appeared in Regan (1991). It is included here with permission of the publisher, *The Collaborative Educator.*

5

Relational Knowing

A Process for
Constructing Knowledge out of Experience

In the preceding chapters, we have described the foundational metaphor of the double helix, which so powerfully suggests that complete understanding requires the contribution of both genders. We have named and defined the five attributes composing the feminist strand of leadership, and we have shown how they bring meaning to our experiences and enrich the quality of school life and work. This description of the contribution of knowledge created from women's experience to school leadership to date is one theme of the story—the product.

In the natural world, the two strands of the double helix are linked by bridges of hydrogen bonds. In the social world, the two strands of the double helix are linked by a process of communication between the masculinist and feminist strands, which we have chosen to call relational knowing.[1] In this chapter, we describe both how we came to understand this communication mode and how it works to bind the separate strands of the helix together into a powerful unit that is greater than the sum of its parts. So now we turn to the second theme of the book—the process. Here we talk not about what we have learned, but about how we have learned it.

We will relate the outline of our journey to new understanding about women as educational leaders. We believe the journey itself, as well as its way stations described in earlier chapters, has value for others interested in learning more about school leadership in general and women's work as educational leaders in particular. Our task is both a retrospective and prospective one; to describe features of the journey that we now recognize, looking back at and reflecting on our earlier experiences; and to foreshadow future way stations. The journey is still under way, and we now expect it to be never ending. However, we are not as blind as we once were to the landscape around us, and so we grasp new understanding more quickly and with greater clarity, as we encounter new features along the way.

Pagano (1990) reminded us that even before women were allowed formal educations, they told stories. In retelling and analyzing our stories we are building a heritage, not claiming originality but claiming as clearly as we can our antecedents and our contemporaries. In doing so, "We make ourselves known to ourselves by making ourselves known to each other" (p. 135). Like Pagano, we make no claim to originality in setting forth new knowledge; instead, we recognize and honor our predecessors and our contemporaries, and in articulating our experience, we hope that it will be a heritage from which the women who follow us will learn and build new knowledge.

As women, we have experienced life below the fault line of the pyramid, where we have formed a congenial community beginning for us with NECEL, which provided us the safe haven in which we have made ourselves known to ourselves by making ourselves known to each other. Our journey has been a telling and sharing of stories, and here we set them down to make ourselves known to others of like mind. Our sense of the ways women lead has gradually evolved as we have practiced our leadership in the education profession and as we have analyzed our thoughts about our experiences with other women working in similar roles.

The Early Stages: Context for
Coming to Understand Relational Knowing

The catalyst for setting these ideas before a public audience grew out of our experience as members of the governing board of NECEL. A brief history of that organization sets the context for our journey. It has been less than two decades since women began to make inroads into the male-dominated career of public school administration. When we personally began to seriously consider careers in leadership positions in the mid-1970s, we found most doors closed and little if any support in our job searches. Our preparation for administrative roles was dominated by male faculties at the colleges and universities where we studied, and we were taught male-based approaches toward administering schools. Those of us who did gain entry into school administration at that time generally found ourselves as solo women stuck in entry-level positions, with little opportunity or encouragement to move up the ladder.

Around the country at that time, business and professional women were forming networks to support, encourage, and mentor other women. A small group of women began meeting in Boston to discuss issues facing them in their job searches or their administrative positions. Out of these meetings the New England Coalition of Educational Leaders was born in 1975. The women who gathered in Boston have seen their vision come to fruition. The New England Coalition has become the Northeast Coalition of Educational Leaders (NECEL), embracing more than 500 women from Maine to Pennsylvania, with a stated mission of promoting women into educational leadership positions and supporting them in those positions. Although these struggles are important in the context of the history of women in school administration and are very much integrated into the whole of our experiences, they are not the focus of this book. The contribution we make is in bringing new understandings of the female experience of administering schools through naming the attributes that define relational leadership. The journey that has led us to this new understanding and to naming the attributes that make relational leadership unique began through the work of the NECEL governing board and later its affiliate members, who articulated and named these attributes through a collaborative process stretching over many years.

During our planning for this book, we were reminded of Robert Frost's poem, "The Road Not Taken." This prompted us to reflect that should we write a poem about roads, it would be titled "The Road Taken, But Not Recognized." The formation of NECEL was the catalyst for the start of our journey, although at that time we were embarked on the road not recognized. For the first 10 years or so, NECEL focused on figuring out the rules of being a school leader. This meant we formed networks because we had heard that's what the old boys do; we dressed for success; we learned and practiced the games our mothers never taught us (Harragan, 1977); and generally we tried to mimic the behavior of the men leaders around us. We knew that the world of school leadership was organized hierarchically, and we were determined to move up the hierarchy. Many of us did. But, just as we did not know at this point that gender is a category of experience, neither did we know that we were mimicking the rules of the role as we found them. One does not question the given until one sees that it has been given.

> In a world where silences and invisibilities abound, how do we begin the process of exposure; recognizing that which is not said and questioning that which is considered right and natural? How do we examine the construction of our inner eye created from those values and beliefs passed on to us through our educational and professional training? (Gosetti, Mohoric, & Rusch, 1991, p. 10)

We believe the answer to this question lies in respectful and ongoing dialogue between and among our contemporaries.

In one of our conversations, Kristen, thinking back to her early years in administration and in doctoral work said,

> I didn't lack confidence. It was just . . . I was too naive. I was still a fish that didn't know there was water, so I didn't know the questions, the content of the curriculum . . . it was all kind of counterintuitive. I was doing what I was taught to do.

At this time in her career, not only were there few of her female contemporaries with whom to share these feelings but at this juncture, she (or they) were being led to believe that their professional education and training were the way it was "supposed" to be.

Lenz and Myerhoff (1985, p. x) made the point that aspects of the culture must be brought to consciousness before they may be examined and possibly revised. In the early years, most of us, like Kristen, were naive about those aspects of the culture that would lead us to the questions we needed to ask in order to examine and possibly revise that culture. We were only doing what we were taught to do, despite our discomfort with some of those practices.

As NECEL passed its 10th birthday, we found our organizational vision changing. Initially, we had seen NECEL's mission as one of assisting aspiring women administrators to learn about the male-based world of school administration, practice skills needed to operate successfully in it, and overcome barriers for moving up its hierarchy. However, as the years have passed and several of us gained substantial experience in school administration, we found ourselves with a vague, unarticulated sense that there was more to this business of being women school administrators than simply gaining entry to, and learning the secrets of, the world of administration. We felt a need to articulate future goals and directions for NECEL, which we knew needed to be substantially different than our original goals, but just how was altogether unclear. We were poised, ready to move from the concrete to the abstract, from the world of relatively unthinking practice to serious reflection about that practice. We wanted to reconceive the vision of NECEL.

In 1985, an English teacher in Helen's school was invited to participate in the Seeking Equity and Educational Diversity (SEED) project directed by Peggy McIntosh of the Center for Research on Women at Wellesley College. In her capacity as principal of the school, Helen was invited, with heads of other schools, to the lecture where she first heard the metaphor of the broken pyramid. Inspired by this talk, she shared her feelings with the NECEL Governing Board, which invited Peggy to lead a year-long series of seminars in 1986 and 1987 for the 15 members of the board to map out a 10-year plan for the future direction of the organization; this became the Future Directions Project.

What came from that project was a clearer sense of purpose for the organization and a gift we had not imagined: the gift of a beginning of understanding school leadership from a feminist perspective. When we began the seminars, we were looking for a product, a plan that would take us along a path that would meet the changing needs of a growing organization. What gradually emerged was process rather than product, a process to define our leadership, as well as a process to nurture and develop the organization. Here we were just beginning to catch on to what Follett (1924) knew decades before us: "There is no result of process, only a moment in process" (p. 60). It would take us about another 6 years to comprehend this idea fully.

As our seminars were concluding in the spring of 1987, Helen wrote in the introduction to the collection of essays the participants produced,

> Perhaps the best way to communicate the essence of what the seminar series has been like is to describe our struggle to give this document a title. Through the first two sessions, no one could name what we were talking about exactly. Attempts to do so trailed off into frustration and nothingness. But, although we couldn't name it, we all sensed it was taking shape. Also we all understood that our inability to name it was significant; so much of what women do and are is unnamed and therefore unvalued. Finally in the third session we hit upon it; collectively we felt the uncomfortable diffuseness crystallize. We believe the name, *Reconceiving Women and Leadership*, conveys two very important ideas. First, women leaders who are so effective through the use of predominantly collaborative strategies have been leading us, although we did not realize it, to reshaped conceptions of both women and leadership; namely, that women are strong leaders and that effective leadership is collaborative. Second, the work of articulating these reconceptions is in process and open to all. (NECEL, 1987)

Narrative, according to Connelly and Clandinin (1988), is the way humans make meaning of experience. By telling and retelling their stories, people "both refigure the past and create purpose in the future. . . . [Narrative is] a kind of life story, larger and more sweeping than the short stories that compose it" (p. 24). The Future Directions Project was our first experience with narrative as a form of knowing. The foundation for our narrative is the stories of our individual experiences, and their retelling led us to making meaning of our own experiences and began the process by which we would consider their meaning in the larger, more sweeping context of educational leadership.

Bruner (1986) posited two modes of cognitive functioning, "two modes of thought, each providing distinctive ways of ordering experience, of constructing reality. . . . Efforts to reduce one mode to another or ignore one at the expense of the other inevitably fail to capture the rich diversity of thought" (pp. 11-12). He wrote that Richard Rorty was probably correct when he characterized the mainstream of Anglo American philosophy as "preoccupied with the epistemological question of how to know truth—which he contrasts with the broader question of how we come to endow experience with meaning, which is the question which preoccupies the poet and the storyteller" (pp. 11-12). Although we did not understand this then, the title for our essays, *Reconceiving Women and Leadership,* which emerged from our conversations, presages an intuitive knowing that we were reconstructing reality. Telling and retelling our stories was leading us to understand gender as a category of experience and the attributes that define those experiences.

Witherell and Noddings (1991) have said that story and narrative are central to the work of educators. They also emphasized the primacy of caring and dialogue in educational practice and asserted that the notion of caring entails a relational notion of self, formed and given meaning in the context of relations with others. Although we make no claims as poets or storytellers of quality, we do see that our small stories, stitched together to form the narrative that is this book, have endowed our experience with meaning. Giving voice to our professional beliefs and practices within the context of caring relationships with one another, we came to understand and then to speak as we are doing here, thus rendering our experience accessible to all.

Over the months of the seminar series, as the stories of our professional lives were unfolding, we found they were becoming interwoven with the stories of our personal lives, and in the unfolding process, we slowly began to comprehend a powerful message: Our approaches to our jobs could not be separated from the core values around which we lived our personal lives. We struggled with identifying what it was that made the way we defined our roles as school leaders, and the ways in which we carried out those roles, different from those of our male colleagues. Emphatically, they were not quantitative differences because we all knew we were working as hard, harder in many cases, than the men with whom we worked. Gradually came the awareness that if we were to continue to discuss women's leadership, we would have to name what it was that we were expressing in a variety of ways, even though it was coming from a common core of feelings and experiences. We have come to realize that women interpret the world through quite different lenses than men. Affected by generations of women's experiences below the fault line, which even the most feminist of men do not fully understand, our practice of school leadership as women is uniquely influenced by our gender. Relational leadership reflects feminine experience.

Almost a year after their conclusion, the Future Directions seminars took on new meaning and vitality as we named and gave definition to attributes we had been struggling to identify through discussion and personal stories. Naming the five feminist attributes was a collaborative effort by members of NECEL. Their codification was first introduced in Cynthia Dubea's presidential address to the membership in October 1989. Bethene LeMahieu is the one of us who gave the attributes their essential definitions, as we have used them in this book. With this step of naming completed, we felt we had come fully to voice by building a firm structure for our understanding that could withstand scrutiny and the strains of rigorous application.

Once we had constructed the new knowledge that our experience had value, that the characteristic attributes that generally distinguish the practice of school leadership by most women from that of most men are five—caring, vision, intuition, collaboration, and courage—we set about testing our new understanding by looking backward over our careers to date. At this point it was the late 1980s, and we had all been practicing administrators for a dozen years or more. The authors were compelled to put into writing the meanings revealed by the stories and experiences of all of these women. Our first thought was to ask individuals to write about their careers using the five attributes as descriptors, but after a year, that approach produced only two essays. Only two of us are now academics, with both the flexibility and expectation that we write as part of our jobs. The rest of us continue in line jobs where the premium is on action, not reflection, and where the immediacy of that action leaves little time or energy for setting those reflections on paper.

By 1991, we knew that we needed another vehicle by which to transport our understanding of the feminist attributes to others. So we two academics decided to create an environment where reflection was possible. We invited our group to a conference where together we could share and write about our understandings. Here we need to tell another story, as it clearly reflects the way in which feminist leaders go about the business of leading. The idea of telling the story occurred to Gwen as she was taking a break from her computer one day when we were in the midst of preparing a paper that preceded this book. She was folding clothes from her dryer when she remembered how we had finally hit upon the idea of a Writers Conference. It was early fall in 1991, when Gwen, after attending a professional meeting, drove the 50 miles to Helen's house to talk about what to do about our determination to write about the feminist attributes and their implications for educational leadership. When she arrived, Helen was folding clothes from her dryer, daughter Katie and her friend were chasing Katie's new chocolate lab puppy around the house, and husband Dick was outside raking the yard. Helen finished folding clothes, made lunch, and we sat and talked for a couple of hours (counting the interruptions) about whether we should abandon our plans for a book or try something new. Finally, and with great feelings of exhilaration, we conceived the plan for what we called a Writers Conference. Two months later, we were at a country inn with a group of seven women who had been involved in the original seminar, conversing, writing, and taping a wealth and richness of material that is now woven throughout this book. The material is gathered from lives lived below the fault (folding clothes, preparing lunch) and lives lived above the fault (organizing and leading a successful and meaningful conference).

Once we were all together at the inn, we found ourselves constructing knowledge once again, more systematically and rapidly than we dared hope. About midway through the second morning, we all experienced a tumultuous moment of joy and insight as we saw that each of us was literally touching her heart. We had been talking for a day and a half about some inner gyroscope that had guided each of us at critical moments in our careers, and unconsciously, but so powerfully, we had arrived together at a gesture that symbolized our emerging understanding of the origin of our career choices. We laughed and cried and joked that although men around us may have gut feelings, we have heartfelt feelings. We exulted in the realization that we had learned yet once again from our intuitions. We are no longer surprised when this occurs, but we are always joyful when it happens.

Next began the analytical work of finding language with which to articulate what we had just experienced. That work led us back to themes from the previous day, and from other times together. Nothing about the work of analysis is linear; the connections we make to previous experience, conversation, and analysis occur seemingly randomly. No doubt this quality of our work of constructing knowledge leads us to find conversation a more congenial medium in the early stages of creating new understanding. It's always possible when speaking to say, "Oh, that reminds me of what we said yesterday about . . . " Text, on the other hand, demands linear sequence; when writing this book, we were forced to make decisions about what we should describe first, then second, and so on. The transition from the fluidity of conversation in which random access to any idea is always possible, to the prescribed sequence of text is difficult but essential, because the precision that writing requires clarifies our meaning further and makes it accessible to others. A desired outcome of this broadened accessibility of our analysis of our experience would be circularity of construction; that is, our spoken thoughts, analyzed and set down for all to share, will result in further conversations and broadened understandings. This process of constructing knowledge has led us to our understanding of what we now have named relational leadership.

It was at this stage of constructing new knowledge that we became aware that what we had originally called a Writers Conference would be more aptly called a Conversers Conference; our thoughts and ideas had emerged from our shared storytelling about our careers, rather than from our writing about them. We also now understand that our storytelling is a form of feminist research that leads us to clarified meaning and knowing. What follows are selections from the richness of thoughts and ideas that emerged from our conversations during those two days at an inn, reported in a generally accurate sequence. Watch the meaning emerge, culminating in the wonderful moment when we realize we are all gesturing to our hearts. We named the process we were living at the moment that had first given us the gift of understanding the feminist attributes of leadership, and at that moment we received the gift of understanding how we came to understand.

Relational Knowing in Action: The Conversers Conference

At the outset of our conference, we had talked about rules. Carla noted that men seem to have at least two, possibly three or four, different rulebooks, and they choose the rulebooks dependent upon the situation in which they find themselves. Kristen extended this idea, noting the separation of the public sphere and the private sphere; the public sphere being predominantly the male sphere. Women, who have been historically confined to the private sphere only, grow into adulthood with only one set of rules, the set that guides life below the fault line according to the values of care and collaboration. As we have moved into the public sphere over the last 20 years, we have taken our rulebooks with us, initially quite ignorant that there is another set of rules operating in that arena and that we are carrying our indigenous rulebook with us into the public sphere.

Like us, many women newly arrived in the public sphere initially mimic the new set of rules they see around them. Many of us, certainly those who call ourselves feminists, return to our original set of rules and begin experimenting with the application of the values of the private sphere (below the fault line) in our new public arena (above the fault line). Because this is a new set of rules never before tried out extensively in the public sphere, the potential effect could be transformational. This, we believe, is the compelling reason why our knowledge constructed from women's experience must be disseminated.

The thread of this point led three of us to note that our earliest visions of our lives consisted of having a life different from the external norms around us. Sarah then suggested that this is different from many men, whose visions of their adult lives are externally defined. Jan fleshed out that idea, saying that an external vision is really a professional identity such as doctor, businessman, or whatever. Sarah added the thought that professional identity shapes the rulebook for conduct in that chosen professional arena, which is fundamentally different from the approach taken by women, whose rulebook for right conduct in life has been forged below the fault line amid values of care and collaboration. The specific outlet in the public arena through which particular women express that set of values is entirely secondary, and almost irrelevant. The key idea, symbolized by the gesture of touching our hearts, is that we have embedded deep within ourselves a set of rules for moral conduct that shapes our practice in the public arena of schools, as contrasted to many men, who seem to learn from the role itself what the rulebook is.

Gregorc (1984; all quotations from p. 5) wrote, "Words such as morality, good, and evil are not commonplace in the lexicon of to-day's school leaders," although he says the allusions are there in those things that concern us, such as commitment to equal educational opportunity, meeting the needs of all children, and so on. He said that the primary reason for not using words such as *morality, good,* and *evil* "appears to be related to our general world view. Schools tend to be viewed as secularized and scientifically based." However, he went on to say that a reconciliation is taking place

> between individuals who study the nature and structure of the ob-jective world and those who study the nature and structure of the subjective world. With this unification comes a blend of the spiri-tual and the material and it is already having a profound effect on the focus, concerns, and subsequent actions in our schools.

Moral leadership is rooted in below-the-fault values, such as car-ing, collaborating, nurturing. The discovery of our deeply held be-liefs was a new discovery for us. What we had not realized was that our common commitment to respect for the dignity and worth of people was a common foundation in which the five attributes are embedded. Here lies the key to mending the rupture of the line of fault in the pyramid. Intuitively we have been seeking to blend the spiritual (the values found below the fault) and the material (values above the fault), of which Gregorc speaks, into the moral leadership symbolized by the two strands of the double helix coming together to form relational leadership.

As we explored our beliefs together, example after example illustrated ways in which our practice is shaped by the five feminist attributes. We have described many of these earlier, illustrating how application of feminist attributes as an interpretive lens for our stories focuses them, highlighting their meaning. Finally, we also came to a qualitatively different understanding, extending us into new territory.

At this Conversers Conference, not only did we name the new knowledge, but we also named the epistemological process by which we had constructed the new knowledge. We articulated for the first time the vehicle in which we had been traveling together for so many years. Looking backward over the two days of the conference, we can see that our intuition had been at work from the beginning leading us to the description of the vehicle. This act of knowing began when we asked the question, "How did you get to this place," meaning "How did you become the administrator you are today?"

Kathleen answered, "At first, I didn't see myself as others saw me." Jennifer encouraged her to elaborate by asking what she thought others saw in her when she did not see herself as a leader. Kathleen responds slowly; the slowness is important because it indicates she is struggling to find words. We are patient, eagerly patient. In a few minutes, Kathleen names two qualities: the abilities to synthesize and to give voice to other people's opinions. As an example, she noted that at a certain point in a contentious faculty meeting, there comes a time when the major points under discussion must be restated so that the discussion can move on to the next step. Kathleen said she always did this. Follett (1924) would call Kathleen skilled at creative integration; we would say she was being visionary.

Kathleen continued,

When I was a teacher, the union representative in our building came to my classroom one day and told me to sign a petition expressing no confidence in our principal. I refused because, no matter what the competence of the principal, I believed this was the wrong way

to proceed. The representative swore at me, telling me I was the
only person in the building who wouldn't sign. Later, at lunch time,
I went into the faculty room and said to everyone, "We are all pro-
fessionals here, and there should be no gang mentality. No one
should be sworn at"; then I sat down. During the rest of the day,
people came up to me quietly, thanking me for speaking out. The
petition died.

This was an act of courage on Kathleen's part. As she finished
speaking of it, Jan noted that Kathleen had not understood the significance of this act until she told the story to us and that this deep-
ening understanding is what is so valuable about this process of our
being together, talking about our lives and work. We all saw this as
a continuation of the naming that had begun in the Future Directions
Project; we were continuing to create knowledge as we talked to one
another.

At another time during the conference, we asked the question,
"What do you know now as a woman administrator that you want
to make sure is passed on to young women following us?" Significantly, the answers to this question reflected all of the feminist attributes, and we revisited the question many times throughout the
conference. We articulated strong feelings of obligation toward pass-
ing on our knowledge and offering support and encouragement to
younger women. Sarah and Jan said they want younger women to
articulate their firmly held beliefs. Jan in particular expressed regret
that she has found the voice with which to express her firmly held
beliefs only recently, at almost the age of 50. Her regret prompted a
discussion about whether firmly held beliefs are a function of living
and maturing, and so early articulation of them is not possible, or
even desirable. Jennifer said she would want young women to learn
to trust their intuition, but she set forth the notion that young women
have not had the experiences and are not developmentally ready to
act on that intuition. Early in their careers their actions are based on
factual knowledge, but they have not yet had the experience to trust
their intuitive knowing. Carla argued against this developmental
perspective, saying that firmly held beliefs are not articulated earlier
by most of us because discussion of them is not part of the norms of
our work. Sarah built on this, suggesting that if we accepted beliefs

as dynamic, then conversation about them would be safe because we wouldn't be held rigidly to our earliest expressions of our beliefs. This led Kristen to suggest that if beliefs were regularly discussed, then they would become part of the creative process, like this conference, and be more widely understood and more available and useful as guides to moral choices. Perhaps, she suggested, if such creative conversation were part of the norms of our work, then maybe others would have the courage to stand up as Kathleen did in the face of the union representative who was pressuring her to act in conflict with her own beliefs.

The conversation continued for some time on these points, ending with the tentative conclusion that earlier articulation of firmly held beliefs can best happen, using Sarah's language, through relationships such as ours, which were born and nurtured in the safe, comfortable community of NECEL. We recognized that it is not enough to hold a belief privately but that it must be tested out through interaction with others. When these beliefs are validated through interaction with others, one gains confidence and becomes ready to assume a public leadership role.

Kathleen was reminded that she was not yet 30 years old when she had her encounter with the browbeating union representative. Retrospectively, she now saw this as a serendipitous early opportunity to put her belief about the worth and dignity of each individual into practice, and she said that the experience of doing so helped her articulate her beliefs even more clearly and moved her toward being ready for a formal leadership role. Not all of us are fortunate enough to have such shaping experiences early in our careers. Sarah saw Kathleen's experience as an example of beliefs coming to be known and validated to their holder through relationship.

Sarah asked us to consider how we can arrange our environment to facilitate the next phase of growth, how we can ensure that it remains possible to continue being visionary. Unpredictably, but so productively, her question started a line of conversation about unhealthy environments. Jennifer identified Kristen's departure from a particular job as an act of courage. Again we saw the power of relationships when Kathleen said that Kristen's act had caused her to reexamine her own life. Nancy described Kristen's school as a toxic environment analogous to toxic environments for children, and because it was beyond Kristen's ability to clean up, leaving was the only thing left to do. Carla also left a toxic environment, but, she said, "It didn't feel like an act of courage at the time." These comments prompted Jan to mention the gyroscope again; Carla and Kristen were being guided by theirs to take self-preserving action.

In a flash, we all realized we were touching our hearts. The metaphor of the gyroscope had taken on a physical, visceral meaning. Here we laughed and cried as Jan described an inner, white circle glowing in each one of us that shapes our life choices. With amazement, and amazement at our amazement, we realized that our conversation was a creative act. By speaking to one another, we create understanding that we then bring back into the active arenas of our lives. For more than 17 years, we have been participants in a cycle of collaborative reflection leading to the construction of understanding, leading in turn to praxis, which in turn creates the experience, which informs another cycle of reflection, and so on. Until this moment, we had understood only the outcomes of our conversation as meaningful; now we understood that the process was the bearer of meaning.

Bruner (1986) wrote that if the language of education is to invite reflection and culture creating, it "must express stance and must invite counter-stance, and in the process leave space for reflection, for meta-cognition" (p. 129). The process of objectifying in language or image, he said, permits us to reach higher ground.

The invitation to participate in the Conversers Conference, although we were not consciously aware of it at the time, was an invitation to participate in the process of reflection and culture creating. Through the reflections on our beliefs and experiences, we were reaching higher ground. The collaborative process had elicited each one's contribution and cultivated an environment in which our intuitions could flourish. We rewarded one another for courageous acts and increased the probability that we will have the strength the next time courage is called for to act according to our deeply held beliefs. Our trust and respect for the opinions of each member, our caring deeply for one another, and our being visionary together enabled the group to formulate new understandings. Each of us would return to her work, apart from one another, encouraged by the new cognitive and affective understandings we developed together, open to the new experiences that will be integrated into this new knowledge base and that will be the source for our new stories when we come together to create new understanding once again.

Connections to Others:
Implications of Naming the Process

Once we had conceptualized the methodology with which we had been making sense of the ruptures in our experiences with the male-based world of school administration around us, we also saw another instance of how we are part of the larger feminist project under way in the world. Harding (1987) offered us characteristics that distinguish illuminating examples of feminist research: new empirical and theoretical resources—women's experiences, research designed for women, and new subject matter of inquiry that locates the researcher in the same critical plane as the overt subject matter. Although it is not for us to claim that our project is illuminating, our work does entail these characteristics. As with the subject matter of our conversations, we have only retrospectively attained the understanding that enables us to feel connected to the methods of inquiry of other women. How it is that we can only understand everything retrospectively is a topic we will address in Chapter 6.

Although we conceptualized our cycle of creating knowledge without awareness of similar processes going on elsewhere, we now see ourselves as an instantiation of Hollingsworth's *relational knowing,* and we have used her phrase to name our process of learning. Coming to situate ourselves within a wider community is an example of the empowerment of naming. Until we named our process, we did not see it, and until we saw it, we could not recognize the work of others similar to our own or realize that others had stumbled upon the same process and had named it.

Hollingsworth (1992a) located relational knowing at the intersection of three bodies of knowledge: theories of social construction of knowledge, theories of feminist epistemologies, and theories of self/other relationships. Hollingsworth's work is an illuminating example of feminist research. We situate her conception of relational knowing within our text to make conscious for our readers how, unknown to us and at separate times and places, we have been constructing new knowledge emerging from the stories women tell about their own lives and experiences. The process of relational knowing gives us a method of inquiry about women that we have until now neither practiced, fully understood, nor appreciated. Relational knowing as articulated by Hollingsworth

> requires careful listening;
>
> involves both instantiation and the reflection on what is known;
>
> cannot be termed *relational knowledge* because of its fluid and present character;
>
> is attentionally generated through a sense of care for self and other;
>
> occurs in the acceptance of where we are now (becoming);
>
> is situated in the larger, social, political world;
>
> occurs more in energy or intuitive perception than in either concrete or abstract form;
>
> evokes past memories of stored knowledge transformed into knowing through not only cognitive, but moral, spiritual, psychological, and physical response; and
>
> allows the teacher to act in an intuitive mode: an involvement of the senses, a commitment and receptivity, a quest for understanding or empathy, and a productive tension between subjective certainty and objective uncertainty.

The moment when we realized with deep emotion that we were all touching our hearts was a quintessential moment of relational knowing. It was a beautiful moment of past memories of stored knowledge transformed into knowing through cognitive, moral, spiritual, psychological, and physical response. The conversation that led up to that moment, beginning some 17 years before, although not concretely about coming to understand relational knowing, was both instantiation as we told our stories and reflection on what is known (for the moment because relational knowing, like vision, really describes an activity, not a product). We are exquisitely careful listeners of one another, enjoying quiet as well as talk. Our stance toward one another is one of care and empathy, as we enjoy both the moments of ambiguity when meaning is under construction, but not yet clear, and the moments of joyous insight when new meaning energetically bursts forth.

In our readings and conversations with others as we wrote this book, we have been struck by the groups we are finding who have experienced, or who are going through, similar processes. Hollingsworth (1992a) described a group of beginning teachers who remained in conversation over a period of 2 years, constructing knowledge together about teaching through relational knowing. Miller (1990) facilitated a 3-year conversation among a group of educators who had been her graduate students, in which the participants researched their own practice; this conversation also evolved into an exercise in relational knowing. Preceding Hollingsworth's work, the term *relational knowing* was not available to Miller, as it was not to us, but, like us, her group discovered it on their own and was sustained and encouraged by its power to "create spaces and find voice." In our own practice, we have each taught (or teach) a course much like the one Miller describes. Graduate students who are professional practicing educators construct research based on a problem taken from their own classroom experiences. Through conversation with their classmates and colleagues at their schools, and their own reflections about the issue, the teachers become experts. This is the empowerment Prawat (1991, p. 739) perceived when he said that changing teacher conversations "with settings," that is, taking an active rather than a passive stance toward their work, will encourage them to be their own experts and overcome their tendency to uncritically accept the knowledge handed down to them from the so-called experts. This, he said, will encourage teachers to find new and effective ways to construct the classroom and workplace environment. Although he does not name it so, Prawat's conversations with self and setting are a form of relational knowing.

The experience meetings that Follett (1924) wrote about are also a form of relational knowing. From the political science perspective from which she wrote, she envisioned experience meeting as an experiment that she believed would enable (i.e., empower) a participant electorate, as distinguished from an electorate whose only function was to grant consent. These meetings would bring together the expert and the people, with the result that

> the experience of the people will change the conclusions of the ex-
> pert while the conclusions of the expert are changing the experience
> of the people; further than that, the people's activity is a response to
> the relating of their own activity to that of the expert. (pp. 216-218)

Here is knowing created through relationship described 60 years ago.

Pagano's (1990) choice of a conversational model, which she maintains requires the self-conscious production, acknowledgment, and celebration of difference (p. xvii), is still another instance of women seeking creative integration of the experience of the world of both genders. Like us, Follett viewed difference as opportunity. Relational knowing is creative conversation open to all who would listen with care, open to those moments of intuitive insight by which we can more tightly knit one strand of the double helix to the other. We have been very comfortable in the separate community we created as the haven we needed from the larger world while we explored the disjuncture between practice in the public sphere of school administration and the below-the-fault values of the private sphere, but now we wish to invite others to join us as full participants in practicing creative conversation to benefit us all.

It is clear, we think, to borrow Nelle Morton's phrase, that the journey is home. As long as we are alive and in relation with one another, joyfully, it will continue. At this historical moment, it is a journey undertaken primarily by women, and many of them do not understand that they are under way. Like us, they are embarked on the road not recognized. Two points are important about this:

1. How do we ensure that others, women and men, join us?
2. Why is it that the existence of this road, and descriptions of way stations others have discovered, are unknown to most of us?

We turn to these questions in the next chapter.

Note

1. *Relational knowing* is a term we first heard used by Sandra Hollingsworth (1992b) in a paper presented to the annual meeting of the American Educational Research Association Special Interest Group: Women and Education.

6

No More Loss

In the Tradition of the Bluestockings, the Langham Place Group, and the Six-Point Group

It has been a revelation to us as we have traveled farther down this road not recognized to discover how worn that road is. But like many paths in the deep woods, which seem to have been left undiscovered, this one too might eventually have been lost in time except for people like ourselves who stumble upon it. Why didn't we know?

"Why Didn't I Know?" is the title of the first chapter in Dale Spender's (1982) book, *Women of Ideas and What Men Have Done to Them.* The origin of her book lies, she said, in her own personal experience in the 1960s, when she felt a compelling need to find out if other women felt and thought as she did in a male-dominated society (p. 2). Her search led her to converse with other women and to read contemporary feminist literature, such as Betty Friedan's *The Feminine Mystique* (1963). She slowly realized that, yes, other women did feel as she did, and what's more, that her feelings of things amiss were not a matter of any personal deficiency on her part, or on the part of women generally.

Next, Dale Spender and others posed the question: Are we the first generation of women to feel this way? The answer to that seemed to be no; there were enough tidbits—vague impressions of the movement for women's suffrage or isolated names like Mary Wollstonecraft—floating about to indicate that other generations of women had also found the world a difficult place. The accepted explanation for the fragmentary nature of this information, Spender realized, was the assertion that women like Wollstonecraft and movements like the suffragettes were rare and outside the norm. These were odd women and thankfully, from the perspective of patriarchal society, there were very few of them (p. 2).

Spender is nothing if not tenacious. She did not accept the standard explanation for the scarcity of information about the attitudes and actions of previous generations of women. Instead, she launched an investigation of her own, which after many years and much diligent and comprehensive research, resulted in her book. Its central thesis is that there have been many, many feminists before our generation. We don't know about them because they have been systematically rendered invisible and/or discredited by the workings of a patriarchal society. She, and we, didn't know because we were not supposed to know (p. 13).

The body of Spender's book is an accounting of the lives and thoughts of the many feminists who have preceded us. Beginning with Aphra Behn in the 16th century, who is thought to be the first woman to support herself through writing, and extending up to our time, the sheer mass of Spender's book (738 pages) prompts the reader to ask herself, Yes, why didn't I know? If Spender's explanation is not correct, what are the other possibilities? Spender pointed out that with each generation, women begin anew, reconstructing a feminist perspective on the world that had been constructed in the preceding generation but not transmitted to the next. In each century, groups of women find each other, coming together with only their personal experience as a benchmark, and discover with joy that other women share their feelings and experiences. In the 18th century, for example, the Bluestockings, a group of wealthy women, used the private space of the salon deliberately to cultivate an intellectual life in violation of the norms of the day. The term *Bluestockings* has endured to our day as a term of derision for privileged women with an unfounded pretension to serious scholarship. According to Spender, such discrediting is a case in point of how patriarchal society systematically discredits feminists (p. 102).

In the 19th century in England, Barbara Bodichon discovered a group of like-minded women as she secured signatures on a petition supporting the Married Women's Property Bill. The women coalesced into a group called the Langham Place Group after their meeting place. They met regularly and branched out into various activities, such as publication of *The Englishwoman's Journal*, a feminist publication in every sense of the term (p. 414).

In our own century, in 1921, Lady Rhondda founded the Six-Point Group, named after the six points it formulated for parliamentary action. The feminist positions of the Six-Point Group appeared in the radical journal *Time and Tide*, which was financially underwritten by Lady Rhondda herself. The journal was published into the 1960s, and the Six-Point Group continued to meet even longer. Its last member, Hazel Hunkins-Hallinan, died in 1982.

It saddens but does not surprise us to realize that even our book has been touched by this process. An engaging and riveting account of the discovery of the double helix was published by James Watson (1968), one of three persons who received the Nobel Prize for this work in 1962. In Watson's book, a woman, Rosy, peers over her spectacles, looking like "the perfect, unadulterated stereotype of the unattractive, rigid, dowdy, aggressive, overbearing, steely, 'unfeminine bluestocking,' the female grotesque we have all been taught either to fear or to despise" (Sayre, 1975, p. 19).

Helen read *The Double Helix* soon after its appearance, but she did not question the representation of Rosy in any way. A chemistry teacher at the time, she reacted with distancing and exception; she was grateful that, although she had majored in chemistry as an undergraduate, she was certainly not the "unfeminine bluestocking" described by Watson. Only years later did she hear vague rumblings that Rosalind Franklin had been a major contributor to the discovery of the double helix and that Watson had seriously understated her contribution in his book. Even at that, Helen did not see that such distortion of a woman's contribution was part of a larger historic pattern.

Given the devaluing of Rosalind Franklin's part in the discovery of the double helix, use of it here in our book as a metaphor to conceptualize and communicate the feminist attributes of leadership and their part in relational leadership is most ironic. Preparation of this book led us to Sayre's retelling of Franklin's part in the double helix story, in *Rosalind Franklin and DNA* (Sayre, 1975). Interestingly, Sayre herself, although she knew Franklin personally, was not immediately troubled by Watson's characterization of her in his book. However, two discrepant facts caught her attention. No one, friend or family, ever used the nickname Rosy to refer to Rosalind, nor did she wear spectacles. Sayre began to inquire and came to the conclusion that Watson consciously misrepresented Rosalind Franklin. Her book explains her reasons for this conclusion, speculates as to his motives, and sets the record straight about Franklin's contribution to the discovery of the double helix. In this case, at least, there has been a response to the devaluing of a woman's ideas.

"The silence of women has been a cumulative process. Conceptually and materially excluded from the production of knowledge, their meanings and explanations have been systematically blocked and their invisibility has been compounded" (Spender, 1987, p. 59). Those of us who founded NECEL in 1975 did not know of the Bluestockings, the Langham Place Group, or the Six-Point Group. We came together with only our own personal experiences as women school administrators as points of reference. We worked initially from an ahistorical and atheoretical perspective because we were ignorant that historical and theoretical frameworks for our experiences existed. Had we known more about our predecessors, perhaps the innocence and naiveté of our beginnings would have been less pronounced. Perhaps we would have arrived at the place of our current understanding many years sooner and so had those years available for other creative efforts.

The joy of previous generations of women in finding like-minded others that Spender describes is much like what we have experienced. We too have drawn support and encouragement from each other as our careers have progressed. And just as the members of the

Bluestockings, the Langham Place Group and the Six-Point Group discussed and wrote in ignorance of the breadth and depth of women's history, so too did we. We thought we were thinking and doing everything for the first time. Such was the legacy of our elite educations, our experience of the world, and the systematic silencing of women's experience.

Spender wrote, "Those who have the power to name the world are in a position to influence reality" (p. 165). Naming the feminist attributes has revealed new possibilities for exerting influence through relational leadership in changing the culture of schools. If we are to realize these possibilities they must be passed on. In our discussion at the Conversers Conference of what we want to pass on to the young women who follow us, Jan spoke passionately of helping them articulate their firmly held beliefs earlier than she has. "I can't articulate it exactly," she said, "but I know I have spent too much time trying to fit into the mold." Jan's comment prompted Kristen to think about our educations, particularly our graduate, professional educations. "Most of what we were taught about the theory and practice of administration," she said,

> was rooted in a patriarchal perspective. As we struggled to master and apply this knowledge base, our development as feminist leaders was actually slowed down. Not only were we not taught that some of our qualities originating in our experiences below the fault are critical to effective administration, the existence of that experience base was never spoken of. For me at least, for most of us in this room, they remained below the level of my consciousness well into my career. We were co-opted by the system as we went through its initiation rites, and we actively, although unconsciously, colluded in our own blindness and ignorance for many years.

Ferguson (1984) would perceive our experience of blindness and ignorance as simply one insignificant instantiation of the effectiveness of bureaucracy in perpetuating its own existence through oppression of the individual.

> The knowledge [that educational institutions] impart to students is fragmented and discontinuous. . . . Nonadministrative goals such

as open-endedness, self-expression, or critique are sacrificed to the
technical requirements of efficient production; in the case of education, the "product" is the administratively socialized and docile
future worker or manager or client with the appropriate technical
and/or bureaucratic skills. . . . The typical socialization process in
our schools prepares individuals simultaneously to participate in
bureaucratically ordered activities and to refrain from compre-
hending the real place of such activities in the technical society.
(pp. 44-45)

We have been both the product, administratively socialized into docile managers, and the instrument of continuing socialization of children and adults who work with us. As both objects and instruments,
we did not comprehend the "real place" of our activities.

In one sense, groups of females over the centuries have been
thinking and doing everything for the first time. Each group has
existed in a particular historical context. The salons of the Bluestockings, where women conducted serious discussions of new discoveries of the day, fit into the pattern appropriate for people of their social
class at the time. The Langham Place Group, operating as it did in
mid-19th-century England, was an activist group supporting
changes in laws regarding property rights of women. The Six-Point
Group was founded in the heady period immediately following the
gaining of suffrage for women, and so it focused on capitalizing on
their new political opportunities.

In the same way, NECEL was formed around issues particular to
its historical period. We were among the few women in school administration. Although we vaguely knew we were among many
similar women's networks forming in the 1970s, we had only the
most tenuous of connections with other such groups in education.
We certainly did not know that we existed in a historical tradition of
feminist groups.

When we entered school administration, many of us experienced
all of the problems related to being the only woman in an administrative position in the district. We encountered problems in being
hired, and we saw discrepancies between what we thought and felt
and what we knew we were supposed to think and feel. We struggled
for language with which to speak, even to each other. There just

weren't words or concepts for our experience. Jennifer noted that Kathleen had begun the story of her move into administration by saying,

> Like so many women, I drifted . . . I was always very clear about what I believed in; now that doesn't mean those beliefs weren't changed and shaped and molded over time as I grew professionally and intellectually, . . . but I think when I look back over time, I didn't view myself as others viewed me and they were pushing me along.

Jennifer viewed Kathleen's perception of drifting and her inability to see the leadership qualities in herself that others saw in her as a consequence of our lack of language for describing our qualities, as well as the loss of women's history, which would connect us to others who shared those qualities. Because we don't conceptualize our qualities, we don't know we have them, don't know they are valuable, and cannot conceive of ourselves as leaders.

Just as our sisters before us joined together to find a congenial group with which to make sense of experience, and with whom one could stand shoulder to shoulder in advocating for change, so too did we come together. Initially we thought the change we were advocating was a breaking down of barriers preventing us from entering or moving up into the world of educational administration. NECEL began with a classic, liberal perspective toward our issue; we simply "wanted in" to an existing system. As our creative work together deepened our understanding, we have come to want to change the system.

The issue that distinguishes NECEL from those women preceding us is the question of women in leadership roles. The structure of modern organizations, of which schools are one form, is a 20th-century phenomenon, and so our sisters were not confronted with the problem of making sense of organizational life as we have been. Now, almost two decades after the founding of our group, we have discovered a language enabling us to articulate a feminist perspective on women in school leadership. We now see that we stand firmly in the tradition of the Bluestockings, the Langham Place Group, and the Six-Point Group.

During our discussion about the formation of firmly held beliefs, Carla suggested that the literature on adult development (see, for example, Knowles, 1973; Levine, 1989) might read altogether differently if we were raised in a different environment. She said,

> If our educations facilitated rather than blocked examination of our feminist qualities, maybe we'd become clearer sooner about what's really important. Maybe we wouldn't spend half a lifetime mustering courage to articulate the uneasy sense that what's around you and what you believe don't match, that that unease doesn't mean something's wrong with you, and luckily (or not, in many cases) eventually finding others in print or in life who share your feelings and beliefs and help you speak out with confidence.

Mary Parker Follett (1868-1933) was a woman who understood many of the concepts we have come to understand. In major works, *The New State* (1920), *Creative Experience* (1924), and *Dynamic Administration, The Collected Papers of Mary Parker Follett* (1940), she wrote about the importance of process over product, the creative opportunity found in difference, the idea of integration as the key to progress, concepts that resonate with many aspects of feminist leadership. We have cited her throughout this book. Yet, Mary Parker Follett is an example of loss. We found her quite by accident by listening to a paper presentation at the annual meeting of Special Interest Group: Research on Women in Education in 1991. In that paper, Gosetti et al. (1991) wrote,

> An obscure reference in a research project on women in leadership led to the work of Mary Parker Follett, a political and business philosopher during the 1920s and 1930s who is still described today as being "the most modern management expert" (Wren, 1987, p. 264). She is credited with being the first writer to present a comprehensive theoretical view of administration of the modern organization. (p. 7)

Evidently, Follett is undergoing somewhat of a rediscovery, but, not for the first time. According to Lyons (1990), "Follett's work has had a curious history, first widely acclaimed, then neglected and yet from time to time rediscovered" (p. 278). We assume it was in one of its undiscovered periods when we were in graduate school, because Follett was not on any of our reading lists in the late 1970s and early 1980s. This pattern does not surprise us; what would have been her influence on our work if we had known about her at the outset? Sadly, we predict that she will be lost again. In our fleeting moments of pessimism, following more persistent moments of optimism when we make the modest assumption that a few others will find us, we expect to be lost too.

We discovered the process of what we have come to know as relational knowing in ignorance of the similar work of Hollingsworth (1992b) and Miller (1990), not because their work has been lost (it's too new for that), but because it is new. Most likely there are other groups, many of whom we hope will discover this book, who have also discovered the power of relational knowing and are living it each day in their work. However, Prawat (1991) labels this "an alternative form of discourse," meaning it is out of the mainstream. The essence of his article is to make a case for the legitimacy of an alternate form of discourse.

The work of feminist scholars is too recent and not yet widely enough known to ensure that a group like ours would be familiar with the concept of relational knowing, even if it were not published simultaneously with our own work. In a sense, Hollingsworth and Miller are lost, lost not in the sense that once they were found and now are gone, but in the sense that their work exists but is not widely known. The important question to ask: Is this simply a matter of time, or this an instance in the making of the devaluing of women's ideas?

We believe that the world of the broken pyramid is crumbling around our ears. Our resolve to disseminate our understanding of the contribution of women to school leadership is rooted in our understanding that the contributions of generations of women before us, who also discovered that knowledge is contained in women's experience, have been destroyed and lost. Throughout this book, we have cited extensively from the works of other women and have set down the words of our colleagues and contemporaries. At times we have paused to consider this, leading to the realization that we have done this because we respect and honor the work of these women. If women can integrate the words and works of other women into their own work and their lives, perhaps what has preceded us and what follows will not be lost. We believe that the price for losing these works yet again is even higher in our generation than it has been in preceding generations. For example, even if we restrict our analysis to schools, we know that schools as they are currently constituted in the hierarchical model, reproducing existing divisions of gender, race and class, are failing dismally to educate many children for productive lives in the 20th century. What good is a position atop a pyramid that is falling over? This notion gives us hope that, unlike our foremothers, perhaps the feminist project, of which our work is but one small part, this time will have lasting impact. In our final chapter, we turn to consideration of how leaders, women and men, in formal and informal ways, can work for change within schools.

7

Conclusion

Relational Leadership for Change

The masculinist strand of the double helix is already well described. This book has emphasized the feminist attributes of leadership in the feminist strand: what they are, how they look in practice, how we came to recognize them, why they are important. However, what about the double helix as a whole? We have said that it is not simply two strands linked together but a functional whole different from either of its two parts. Relational leadership is this functional whole—an integrative (both/and) form of leadership created through the seamless integration of both sets of attributes.

Although we know that relational leaders exist (we think of ourselves as such), to our knowledge, no one, including ourselves, has examined leadership through this lens. That is a project for the future, which will require the efforts of scholars familiar with the classical and emerging literature on leadership, as well as reflective practitioners of both genders who have consciously integrated masculinist and feminist attributes of leadership in practice. In our opinion, much groundwork must be laid before this project is even possible. Many more people must understand and practice the feminist attributes of leadership before analysis of relational leadership can even be conceived.

In the balance of this chapter, we examine barriers that operate to keep the feminist attributes of leadership invisible, unspoken, and therefore inaccessible to all people. Next, we counter with stories of small projects undertaken by each of us, and others we have read about, that indicate that the barriers are not insurmountable. Finally, we end with an invitation to all to form groups devoted to relational knowing, the bridge between the feminist and masculinist strands. Such groups can lead us to understanding of the feminist attributes of leadership, and from there to exploration of relational leadership as a way for women and men to work together for change.

Weiler (1988), in her book *Women Teaching for Change*, synthesized critical theory and feminist theory to suggest how people situated within schools can actively resist the structural and institutional forces that work to reproduce existing conditions in which all of us, women and men alike, are rendered powerless to address the deficiencies of schools. In their introduction to her book, Henry A. Giroux and Paulo Freire wrote that

> Weiler rejects the notion that reproduction and resistance are dichotomous social practices; she argues instead that they are mutually informing relations of contradiction that produce forms of social and moral governance on the one hand, and the regulations of subjects, texts, and subjectivities on the other. This is an important conceptual advance. . . . Around and within those particular social forms, relations of power, and institutional configurations of schooling, the women in her book fight to reclaim the moral and politically regulated terrains of history, space, time, textuality, desire, and subjectivity. (p. x)

We are embedded within the culture of schooling, and we choose to remain there. However, like the teachers whose teaching for change Weiler describes, we see the possibility for constructive resistance from the inside. We see that the more articulate we become, the more capable and confident we become about resistance. We see possibilities for resistance all around us, projects possible for both women and men. Emanating from firmly held beliefs involving respect for the dignity and worth of others, we believe relational leadership is moral leadership. The present state of American education cries out for transformational change, led by any and all people who have a vision of how schools can be organized more humanely and productively, with the learning of all children as the central principle. What is needed is for others to see the possibilities inherent in relational leadership; the possibilities for the evolutionary change inherent within it, which has the power to "reclaim the moral and politically regulated terrains of history, space, time, textuality, desire, and subjectivity."

From the beginning, we have asserted that knowledge created from women's experience is accessible to both women and men, in the same way that knowledge created from men's experience became accessible to women once they had access to education. However, given the pervasiveness of the broken pyramid as the prevailing metaphor of our culture, the change process by which women and men will come to understand the knowledge created from women's experience and the process of relational knowing through which it has been created will be very different. Women approach this task from the perspective of those below the fault line, with the clear understanding of life above the fault line that is essential for survival by the oppressed. This knowledge is almost universally held by women, even if they do not see the fault line itself.

Most men, on the other hand, having been raised to life above the fault line, do not know of the existence of the world below the fault line. They are ignorant of the world of women and people of color in a way that women are not ignorant of their world. This difference has consequences for how each gender can approach the project of changing from an understanding of the world based on the metaphor of the broken pyramid to an understanding of the world based on the metaphor of the double helix. The starting point for each gender, however, will be the same.

Points of Rupture:
Guilt or Anger, Collaboration

Bureaucracy does not discriminate by gender, oppressing women but not men. All people living in schools inhabit this quint-essentially bureaucratic organization, which is the classic form of the broken pyramid. This means that there must exist a line of fault for men like the one that exists for women—occurring when they discover "a point of rupture in their experience [as men] within social forms of consciousness" (Smith, 1987, p. 49). This discovery of a line of fault is a common experience for both women and men in schools. Teachers and administrators of both genders experience the feelings of powerlessness and impotence that are characteristic of lower positions in bureaucratic structures. This is a common experience that can be a common ground for articulating the broken pyramid, naming its deficiencies, and becoming ready to understand the implications of the double helix. However, realization of these implications leads to the difference in experience.

Located above the fault of the broken pyramid because of their gender, men must find it far more difficult, at least consciously, to realize that school bureaucracy has effectively pushed them down below the fault line with the rest of us. Such a recognition might appear initially to extract a great price. Comprehension of the broken pyramid as a metaphor of culture leads inevitably to the realization that, as a man, the person has been a part of the oppression of women, consciously or unconsciously. This evokes guilt, which is painful to experience and difficult to endure (McIntosh, 1988). It is far easier not to see than to see. We understand and empathize with the inability, unwillingness, and resistance of many men to confront the point of rupture in their experience, because women too must endure painful feelings to acknowledge the existence of the broken pyramid.

As women, the experience of a point of rupture first leads to feelings of denial—maybe other women have been pushed down below the fault line, but I have not experienced anything like that. This has certainly been the reaction of most of us during our journey to current understanding. However, slowly but inexorably, one sees more and more clearly, so that inevitably the day arrives when one realizes that one is not the exception but has been the object of dis-

crimination along with other women. This evokes anger, the parallel
stage to feelings of guilt among men. These feelings are as disturbing
as guilt feelings are painful. As women, many of us are as unwilling
or unable to deal with this experience as are men faced with the guilt
accompanying the understanding of patriarchy as a system. Here is
another common experience; it is easier for both genders not to see
than to see.

Among both genders, however, there are those of us who perse-
vere through the hard stuff, to arrive mutually at a place where together we want to work constructively for change. Here is the place
to learn about the double helix, to cultivate appreciation through it
for knowledge constructed from women's experience as well as
men's, to move on to developing an understanding of relational leadership; first, by receiving knowledge about the attributes composing
the feminist strand; next, by looking for examples of the feminist
attributes of leadership already in practice but unnoticed because
unnamed; and finally, by creating projects for exerting relational
leadership more often, more consciously, in more situations. Collaboration among women and men sharing a joint vision of how schools
can be organized differently becomes possible.

We are encouraged about the possibilities of women and men
administering together for change. Just as we were completing this
book, we came upon concrete instances of men speaking the mother
tongue. In a piece whose title suggests an oxymoron, "Power and
Caring," George Noblit (1993) wrote about a feminist attribute of
leadership: care, as we understand it. Here is a man writing of an
instance of feminist praxis in which a real experience has "rendered
what [he] knew obsolete" (p. 32). Here is a man refining his admit-
tedly male concepts of power to assimilate his new understandings
of care as power. Here is a man grounding his new understanding in
feminist literature, specifically Gilligan (1982) and Noddings (1984).

Rosiek (1994) wrote about care as an organizing principle for
teaching classroom management to future teachers. In his article
"Caring, Classroom Management, and Teacher Education: The Need
for Case Study and Narrative Methods," he tells the poignant story
of his encounter with Ramone. In a moment of high tension as
Ramone was refusing to take his seat, another male student asked
Ramone, "What are you doing?" Then the student added, "He's

(Roseik, the teacher) good to us." Something in Ramone shifted, "Yeah, I know." Ramone did take his seat, and the potential for confrontation dissipated. Rosiek concludes his article by saying that one of the alternative sources to rational principle as the source of theory for classroom management "is a compassionate and caring ethic which uses reason as a tool, not as a guiding principle" (pp. 27-29). When reminded of the care he had received, Ramone decided against aggression.

Here are two instances of men crossing the fault line in the opposite direction, achieving creative integration of a masculinist and feminist perspective in the image of the double helix (see also Starrat, 1991). Here is cause for hope that the transformation of the practice of leadership we envision may actually happen through the combined efforts of women and men coming sometimes separately, sometimes together, to an understanding of the feminist attributes of leadership.

Pointing the Way:
The Importance of Role Models

"Patriarchy," says Spender (1987),

> is an interlocking system with its psychological and material components, and while women's consciousness may indicate the desirability and even necessity of practicing "disagreeableness" in order to undermine patriarchy, material circumstances may prevent them from doing so. It was a tenet of the nineteenth-century (and early twentieth-century) women's movement, that there could be no autonomy for women until women were economically independent, and it is a tenet that is no less relevant today than it was then. (p. 4)

In an earlier chapter we referred to Nancy's observation that she has noticed a fundamental change in a group when the number of women reaches a critical proportion—competitive behavior recedes and collaboration becomes possible. In greater numbers than ever, women in leadership positions are becoming economically inde-

pendent, and although we certainly have not yet reached critical pro-
portions, our presence in greater numbers in school leadership positions can catalyze changes in the ways schools are administered.

A leadership study conducted by Judy B. Rosener and her asso-
ciates at the University of California, McAllister and Stephens (1990),
states that "women do lead differently than men and . . . their type
of leadership is increasingly effective. It is transformational leadership which is often associated with the success of future organizations." We suggest that at this early stage in the development of
relational leadership it is more likely that women rather than men
will develop new understandings first, and so as they increase in
numbers in schools, they increase the possibility that others will experience their own points of rupture and begin their journeys to understanding relational leadership. We have just begun ourselves to
think about the wider consequences of our presence in our schools.

We began the second day of the Conversers Conference by asking
the question, "What impact does implementation of the feminist attributes of leadership have on your school/district?" We were silent
for a period as each of us thought and wrote. Kathleen chronicled
how she had thought about the question. She began by considering
leadership, which led her to think that all leaders have an impact on
the people around them, which in turn made her pessimistic, because
such an impact alone will not bring about the major transformation
of schools that we seek. Then her thoughts switched to teaching, and
she began to consider the strategies used by the best of us out there
now. She thought of the whole language method of literacy acquisi-
tion, which dignifies the child's own experience; of cooperative learning, which teaches children the power of collaboration; of interdis-
ciplinary teaching, exemplified by a schoolwide unit on the 1920s
recently taught in the middle school in her district, which overcomes
the fragmentary nature of education. "I hope," she said,

> that these children are growing up differently because of the differ-
> ent pedagogical strategies they are meeting in school. I see an align-
> ment between these new strategies for teaching and the feminist
> attributes of leadership. Hopefully the combined influence of both
> will move out into the world with the children.

Nancy and Sarah immediately saw the implications of Kathleen's point. They noted that these instructional strategies are not only about acquiring facts, but they can empower children to interact differently with the world. Here is a point of resistance.

Kathleen also spoke of the insistent requests she receives from parents for parent education—no matter what the socioeconomic status of the district. Now she responds to these requests by teaching parents how to help their children be successful with the new pedagogical strategies, because doing so fosters the same qualities in children that direct parent education emphasizes—taking responsibility for one's own learning and behavior, being a productive member of a group, using intuition, being a caring community member. None of these qualities were fostered in the old competitive classroom, where conversation and cooperation between and among students was forbidden. Kathleen's point prompted Kristen to think of the standards published by the National Council of Teachers of Mathematics (1989), and the "habits of mind" advocated by the American Association for the Advancement of Science. These two academic groups also value the qualities embedded in new pedagogical strategies and entailed in the practice of relational leadership. Here are other points of resistance.

Susan's stories of the initiatives she undertook as a young woman in her first principalship are points of resistance. She modeled behavior that encouraged the women and men working with her to forge ahead with programs that "a lot of people in the community thought were a bad idea." Recently, reflecting on the feminist attributes, we agreed that this was the kind of risk we must take for the good of the students in our care. Susan said she knew if her plans backfired, "I was the one who would have her neck in the sling. I was the one behind the scenes. They [other team members] were the ones who got the glory, but if it backfired, I was the one who would get it." Susan was willing to confront the resistance of the people who thought the programs were a bad idea and to risk failure, if she could make changes not only in programs but in attitudes that would ultimately benefit the school and the wider community as well.

Susan's comments reminded us of a keynote address Dr. Effie Jones gave at a NECEL conference in 1987. At that time, Effie was the

Associate Executive Director for Minority Affairs for the American Association of School Administrators (AASA). It was under her direction that Project Aware was begun in the mid-1970s to provide encouragement and support for the development across the country of organizations like NECEL. Effie wore a turtle pin on her lapel. To illustrate her remarks to us about the necessity of taking risks in our careers, Effie explained why she wears the pin. Although we can't be sure of her exact words, we remember clearly their significance. Her message was: "The turtle must stick out its neck to make progress. It takes the risk of losing its tail and its neck when it crosses the road." We are certain that as a woman of color, Effie took many risks in her career and emerged as a respected and admired leader. She was a role model for us and, along with Peggy McIntosh, pointed the way.

Helen Regan (1995)[1] has written about the implications of the metaphor of the double helix for school organizations. She specifically addressed the areas of curriculum, teaching and learning, decision making, assessment, supervision and staff development, and organization of space and time. She envisions a utopian world of schools constructed in the image of the double helix. Here we reprint portions of her vision of such a construction:

1. The curriculum would be a broadly stated set of outcomes including both elements of the canon of the either/or strand and new elements from the both/and strand of the double helix. This curriculum would be interpreted in specific classrooms to reflect the interest and experience of the particular learners, serving as window and mirror for all.

2. Learning would be conceptualized as a construction of personal meaning by learners. Teachers would assist through use of a pedagogy that elicits the voice of each learner and draws on the experience of learners as text.

3. Decisions about the organization of a school would be made collaboratively, drawing on the knowledge and experience of all roles, and seeking both the voice of intuition and reason.

4. Assessment would focus on student outcomes with the understanding that complete assessment of learnings of both the either/or strand and the both/and strand require both traditional objective, decontextualized measures as well as subjective, situated measures.

5. Assessment of teachers, with supervisory help, would be done of novice teachers and those who are slow to develop judgment, using external standards.

6. For those teachers whose professional judgments have matured, the focus of assessment would shift from assessment of them to assessments of student learning.

7. Supervision and staff development would focus on issues raised by teachers as they consider the results of their assessment of student learning.

8. Space and time would be organized flexibly, enabling teachers to interact extensively with each other and with administrators.

Schools organized with these characteristics would give formal expression to the both/and qualities of caring, collaboration, intuition, vision, and courage. They would draw on the totality of human experience, facilitating movement of each person back and forth from one strand of the double helix to another. In and of themselves, they would be the enactment of a vision of how schools could be otherwise than they are (Regan, 1995).

Sarah used the parable of the sheepdogs to express her conception of how leaders work effectively for change. The dog leads the pack to the gate of the pen, getting them right where she wants them, and then falls to the rear of the pack so the sheep burst through the gate without the dog in sight, thinking they got home by themselves. This is the way we work, whether we are making eucalyptus wreaths, hiring consultants to assist in team building, or beginning Planning and Placement Team meetings by saying, "If this were our child, what would we want?" We are rarely obvious at the head of the pack; rather we work consistently to have the sheep burst through the gate willingly, believing in their deepest hearts that this is where they belong. In this case, the new place where the sheep have arrived belongs to them, and they will tend it.

Like many analogies, this one can misinform as well as inform. Sheep have reputations as being singularly unintelligent animals, but in no way do we wish to suggest that the teachers and children with whom we work are like sheep in this way. Rather we wish to suggest that implementation of the feminist attributes in our practice of leading with real people in the most liberating sense makes possible the free choice to burst through the gate on one's own. The leader has led the sheep to the gate, but the choice to enter is not forced.

Possibilities of acting as a sheepdog are open to all. Leadership, as we have defined it, is not limited to formal position. What is required is the willingness to act on one's beliefs. Kathleen says, "I'm not a formal leader every day in my district. Sometimes I follow, if that meets the needs of others, or when others have knowledge and experience I lack. However, I always have the big picture in my mind." In most public statements and in her daily interactions, Kathleen models flattening of the pyramid and broadening of its base; she works consciously to fashion a double helix. This is the sheep dog working from knowledge of the home pen over the next hill; this is the leader empowering others.

Astin and Leland (1991) quoted Gerda Lerner on the feminist process of change: "First there is an awareness of wrong, then a sense of sisterhood develops, followed by the autonomous definition of goals and strategies for change, and finally, an alternative vision for the future emerges" (p. 117). Each step of our journey to a new understanding of leadership has followed Lerner's feminist process of change. As novice school leaders, we became aware of the wrong; the dissonance within ourselves told us the model given us for administering was contrary to our own firmly held beliefs. We came together in NECEL to effect change, and through this sisterhood we collaborated to define goals and strategies for changing what we knew needed to be changed. At this moment we share a vision for change, and we now feel empowered to share our vision with the wider world. Through our writing and our work, we hope we are pointing the way for others to examine and follow their firmly held beliefs.

Our development as leaders will never be complete. Relational leadership is dynamic by its very nature. Its nature is entailed in being visionary; we are constantly working with others to solve problems in creative ways, an act that brings new knowledge to us all. Conception of leadership as a formal role governed by a set of rules renders development irrelevant. It prevents the leader from being visionary, forcing him or her to remain perched atop the pyramid, posturing as omniscient and omnipotent. This static conception of leadership robs us of the power of collaboration and interrupts the cycle of relational knowing. The question is, therefore, how to nourish the dynamic nature of relational leadership and how to encourage others to participate. This is the gift of the process, relational knowing, consciously experienced.

Relational Knowing:
A Process for Women and Men Learning Together

To become a sheepdog, what is necessary is the critical understanding of the feminist attributes embedded in relational leadership; their implementation creates points of resistance. To understand the model of relational leadership, at this historical moment, one must be open to learning from women's experience. To learn from women's experience, one needs a congenial group, about half of whom should be women, at least initially, with whom one can engage in relational knowing. To engage in relational knowing, one must be committed to serious reflection about one's practice, willing to engage in respectful dialogue with both men and women, open to seeing the many levels of its meaning, and ready to act on that new meaning as one returns to the world of practice.

Alison Jagger (1983) wrote,

> What I most treasure about feminist thought, then, is that although it has a beginning, it has no end, and because it has no predetermined end, feminist thought permits each woman to think her own thoughts. Apparently, not the truth, but the truths are setting women free. (p. 238)

When we began this book, we did not realize that it had no end, nor did we realize it had its beginnings nearly two decades ago. During the Conversers Conference, Sarah was insistent that we stress that this is a process. Intuitively she understood Mary Parker Follett's "whole a-making" and her contention that there is no result of a process, only a moment in process. We now understand this as well; this is our moment in process. The experience of integrating the metaphor of the pyramid with the metaphor of the double helix is leading us to a new position, a new whole, that is a whole-a-making. This process on which we have embarked has given us the freedom to take our understanding of leadership to a new dimension: relational leadership, a new model of leadership distinguished from the traditional models by the inclusion of the feminist attributes of collaboration, caring, courage, intuition, and vision.

In addition to our experience of relational knowing in the sheltered environment of NECEL, we have described in this book several other such groups that have functioned together to develop knowledge out of women's experience over a period of time. There are undoubtedly others, probably functioning without knowledge that other congenial groups exist as well. One of the messages we want you to take from this book is encouragement to start these groups purposefully, to invite women and men to come together in respectful dialogue and explore the world as we might construct it in the image of the double helix. We are hopeful that as we women learn to articulate and to value the attributes that are the essence of our authentic selves, we will take the risks required to share our knowledge with others, both women and men, and enter into conversations that, although we may not always agree, will be creative and respectful of the values located in each strand, feminist and masculinist, of the double helix. We believe that the more we converse with each other, the more common ground we will find, and, in so doing, we can begin to bond the double helix into a new and stronger form, the transformational model of relational leadership. Our work to date has focused on articulation of the attributes of the feminist strand of the double helix. What future groups will do, we believe, as they practice relational knowing, is articulate the nature of the double helix as a complete entity. This is the next whole-a-making; its product will be understanding of relational leadership, fully illustrated by stories of women and men who have successfully integrated the feminist and masculinist strands in practice.

The Legacy of the Double Helix

From our experience, we are completely aware of the consequences inherent in the structure of school bureaucracies and agree with Ferguson (1984), who contends that bureaucracies have severe consequences for all of its occupants, both men and women. She maintains that bureaucratic domination is oppressive and has the power to "both suppress and produce its victims . . . [It] is repressive in clear and definable ways; it does cognitive and affective damage to its victims" (p. 90). We would extend this to include the children in our schools, who are ultimately the victims in a bureaucratically structured system of education.

However, despite our momentary flashes of pessimism, we believe that the underlying message of our narrative, for both women and men, is one of hope and optimism. We agree with Weiler (1988) that teaching and administering for change are possible; in fact, we believe they are our moral obligation. We know that engaging in them has led us to fulfill the goal Jan set for herself early in life, "to have fun and interesting lives in which we have made a difference in other people's lives." We believe the attributes that characterize relational leadership can transform the educational institution as we know it. To do this we must all find our own points of resistance to help bring about such a transformation in a school system we know to be crumbling beneath the weight of the bureaucratic structure above the fault line of the pyramid. Our points of resistance are those that allow us to work within the system, not counter to it.

Smith (1990) warns us of the danger of "institutional capture." She says that although the creation of a public discourse among women is a major achievement, "it has not been made without the costs of an accommodation to the ruling apparatus" (p. 220). We have tried to contribute to this discourse, and we have tried to indicate the relevance of its form and substance to men, as well as women. However, we are aware of accommodations to the "ruling apparatus" we have made along the way and will make in the future. That does not mean that we believe we must "go along to get along," only that we recognize there are accommodations that must be made while we forge our points of resistance. Weiler gives us hope that such accommodation, essential to survival, is not necessarily fatal. Imperfectly, but continuously, we have located points for resistance. Nourished by our relations with one another, empowered by the understanding wrought together, we continue to administer for change and hope we have pointed the way for others to do so as well.

As we have come to our understanding of this new model of leadership, we note that the implications of the concept of the double helix, with its feminist and masculinist strands linked together through the process of relational knowing to form the practice and theory of relational leadership, exceed the boundaries of education. Although the ideas of this book clearly emanate from our experiences as educational leaders, we suggest that many organizations could profitably consider the question of what can be learned from consideration of the experience of women as leaders. In all fields, men and women need to work together, first by sharing stories of experiences to ensure that the perspectives of both genders are available for interpretation and instruction. Undoubtedly, candid discussion of differing perspectives can lead to conflict, but this conflict need not be paralyzing or destructive. Creative controversy, resolved by a commitment to dialogue grounded in the belief that each gender has something of value to say to the other, can lead to enriched understanding and practice of leadership in any field.

We hope that the legacy of the double helix, the union of the masculinist and feminist strands of leadership, will be to embolden men and women to heed the nagging voice located at the disjuncture of their experiences and dream of the possibilities that can come from the strength and wholeness inherent in this union. And finally, we hope we have encouraged our readers to reach out to one another and begin the inquiry that will lead to understanding, developing, and practicing relational leadership in behalf of themselves and the children and adults entrusted to them.

Councils

(for two voices, female and male)

> ♀ *We must sit down*
> *and reason together.*
> *We must sit down.*
> *Men standing want to hold forth.*
> *They rain down on faces lifted.*

> ♂ *We must sit down on the floor*
> *on the earth*
> *on stones and mats and blankets.*

There must be no front to the speaking
no platform, no rostrum,
no stage or table.
We will not crane
to see who is speaking.

♀ *Perhaps we should sit in the dark.*
In the dark we could utter our feelings.
In the dark we could propose
and describe and suggest.

♂ *In the dark we could not see who speaks*
and only the words
would say what they say.

♀ *Thus saying what we feel and what we want,*
what we fear for ourselves and each other
into the dark, perhaps we could begin
to begin to listen.

♂ *Perhaps we should talk in groups*
small enough for everyone to speak.

♀ *Perhaps we should start by speaking softly.*
The women must learn to dare to speak.

♂ *The men must bother to listen.*

♀ *The women must learn to say, I think this is so.*

♂ *The men must learn to stop dancing solos on the ceiling.*
After each speaks, she or he
will repeat a ritual phrase:

♂ & ♀ *It is not I who speaks but the wind.*
Wind blows through me.
Long after me, is the wind.

From *Circles on the Water,*
Marge Piercy[2]

Notes

1. Material from this essay is reprinted by permission of the State University of New York Press.

2. Piercy, Marge. (1982). *Circles on the Water: Selected Poems of Marge Piercy.* New York: Alfred A. Knopf. Reprinted with permission.

References

Astin, Helen S., & Leland, Carol. (1991). *Women of influence, women of vision: A cross-generational study of leaders and social change*. San Francisco: Jossey-Bass.

Beck, Lynn G. (1992). Meeting the challenge of the future: The place of a caring ethic in educational administration. *American Journal of Education, 100*, 454-496.

Belenky, Mary Field, Clinchy, Blythe McVicker, Goldberger, Nancy Rule, & Tarule, Jill Mattuck. (1986). *Women's way of knowing*. New York: Basic Books.

Bennis, Warren G. (1984). *Leadership and organizational culture: New perspectives on administrative theory and practice*. Urbana: University of Illinois Press.

Bennis, Warren G. (1990). *Why leaders can't lead: The unconscious conspiracy*. San Francisco: Jossey-Bass.

Biklen, Sari, & Branigan, Marilyn (Eds). (1980). *Women and educational leadership*. Lexington, MA: D. C. Heath.

Brooks, Gwen H. (1980). *A phenomenological study of adult developmental patterns of women educational leaders*. Unpublished doctoral dissertation, University of Connecticut, Storrs.

Bruner, Jerome. (1986). *Actual minds, possible worlds*. Cambridge, MA: Harvard University Press.

Connelly, F. Michael, & Clandinin, Jean D. (1988). *Teachers as curriculum planners. Narratives of experience*. New York: Teachers College Press.

Deal, Terrence E. (1982). *Corporate cultures: The rites and rituals of corporate life*. Reading, MA: Addison-Wesley.

Drucker, Peter F. (1954). *The practice of management*. New York: Harper.

Drucker, Peter F. (1990). *Managing the non-profit organization: Principles and practices*. New York: HarperCollins.

Edson, Sakre Kennington. (1988). *Pushing the limits. The female administrative aspirant*. Albany: State University of New York Press.

Ferguson, Kathy. (1984). *The feminist case against bureaucracy*. Philadelphia: Temple University Press.

Follett, Mary Parker. (1920). *The new state*. New York: Longman, Green.

Follett, Mary Parker. (1924). *Creative experience*. New York: Longman, Green.

Follett, Mary Parker. (1940). *Dynamic administration: The collected papers of Mary Parker Follett* (H. C. Metcalf & L. Urwick, Eds.). New York: Harper.

Friedan, Betty. (1963). *The feminine mystique*. New York: Norton.

Gilligan, Carol. (1982). *In a different voice: Psychological theory and women's development*. Cambridge, MA: Harvard University Press.

Gosetti, Penny Poplin, Mohoric, Marge, & Rusch, Edith. (1991). *The social construction of leadership: Theory to praxis*. Paper presented at the annual meeting of the American Educational Research Association Special Interest Group: Research on Women and Education.

Gregorc, Anthony F. (1984). Emergence of moral leadership: Curriculum in context. *Washington State Association for Supervision and Curriculum Development, 12*, 2.

Harding, Sandra. (1987). *Feminism and methodology*. Bloomington: Indiana University Press.

Harragan, Betty. (1977). *Games mother never taught you*. New York: Warner.

Helgesen, Sally. (1990). *The female advantage: Women's ways of leading*. New York: Doubleday.

Hollingsworth, Sandra. (1992a). Learning to teach through collaborative conversation: A feminist approach. *American Educational Research Journal, 29*, 371-402.

Hollingsworth, Sandra. (1992b). *Relational knowing, "gendered experience," and teaching urban schools*. Paper presented at the annual meeting of the American Educational Research Association Special Interest Group: Research on Women and Education.

Jagger, Alison. (1983). *Feminist politics and human nature*. New Jersey: Roman & Allanheld.

Knowles, M. (1973). *The adult learner: A neglected species*. Houston, TX: Gulf.

LeMahieu, Bethene. (1993). Endings, emptiness, and new beginnings. *Voices of NECEL* (Vol. 1, pp. 3-5). Sudbury, MA: NECEL.

Lenz, Elinor, & Myerhoff, Barbara. (1985). *The feminization of America*. Los Angeles: Jeremy P. Tarcher.

Levine, Sarah L. (1989). *Promoting adult growth in schools: The promise of professional development*. Boston: Allyn & Bacon.

Lyons, Nona P. (1990). Visions and competencies: An educational agenda for exploring ethical and intellectual dimensions of decision-making and conflict negotiation. In J. Antler & S. Biklen (Eds.), *Changing education, women as radicals and conservators* (pp. 277-294). Albany: State University of New York Press.

Martin, Jane Roland. (1985). *Reclaiming a conversation: The ideal of an educated woman*. New Haven, CT: Yale University Press.

McIntosh, Peggy. (1983). *Interactive phases of curriculum re-vision: A feminist perspective* (Working Paper No. 124). Wellesley, MA: Center for Research on Women.

McIntosh, Peggy. (1988). *White privilege and male privilege: A personal account of coming to see correspondences through work on women's studies* (Working Paper No. 189). Wellesley, MA: Center for Research on Women.

Miller, Janet L. (1990). *Creating spaces and finding voices: Teachers collaborating for empowerment*. Albany: State University of New York Press.

Mintzberg, Henry. (1989). *Mintzberg on management: Inside our strange world of organizations*. New York: Free Press.

Morton, Nelle. (1985). *The journey is home*. Boston: Beacon Press.

Moyers, Bill. (1993). *Healing and mind*. New York: Doubleday.

National Council of Teachers of Mathematics. (1989). *Professional standards for teaching mathematics*. Reston, VA: Author.

Noblit, George W. (1993). Power and caring. *American Educational Research Journal, 30*(1), 23-38.

Noddings, Nel. (1984). *Caring: A feminine approach to ethics and moral education.* Berkeley: University of California Press.

Noddings, Nel, & Shore, Paul J. (1984). *Awakening the inner eye: Intuition in education.* New York: Teachers College Press.

Northeast Coalition of Educational Leaders (NECEL). (1987). *Toward reconceiving women and leadership.* Unpublished essays, NECEL, Sudbury, MA.

Pagano, Jo Anne. (1990). *Exiles and communities: Teaching in the patriarchal wilderness.* Albany: State University of New York Press.

Peters, Thomas J., & Waterman, Robert H., Jr. (1982). *In search of excellence: Lessons from America's best-run companies.* New York: Harper & Row.

Prawat, Richard. (1991). Conversations with self and settings: A framework for thinking about teacher empowerment. *American Educational Research Journal, 28,* 737-758.

Regan, Helen B. (1990a). Not for women only: School administration as a feminist activity. *Teachers College Record, 91,* 565-577.

Regan, Helen B. (1990b). Using metaphor to establish teacher-principal collaboration. *Holistic Education Review, 31*(1), 22-24.

Regan, Helen B. (1991). Teacher-principal collaboration. *The Collaborative Educator, 5*(4), 4-5.

Regan, Helen B. (1995). In the image of the double helix: A reconstruction of schooling. In D. Dunlap & P. Schmuck (Eds.), *Women leading in education: An agenda for the 21st century* (pp. 407-422). Albany: State University of New York Press.

Rosener, Judy B., McAllister, Daniel J., & Stephens, Gregory K. (1990, July). *Leadership study: The Women's Forum.* Unpublished manuscript, University of California, Irvine.

Rosiek, Jerry. (1994). Caring, classroom management, and teacher education: The need for case study and narrative methods. *Teaching Education, 6*(1), 21-30.

Sayre, Anne. (1975). *Rosalind Franklin and DNA.* New York: Norton.

Schein, Edgar. (1985). *Organizational culture and leadership.* San Francisco: Jossey-Bass.

Senge, Peter M. (1990). *The fifth discipline.* New York: Doubleday.

Sergiovanni, Thomas J. (1984). *Leadership and organizational culture: New perspectives on administrative theory and practice.* Urbana: University of Illinois Press.

Sergiovanni, Thomas J. (1992). *Moral leadership: Getting to the heart of school improvement.* San Francisco: Jossey-Bass.

Shakeshaft, Charol. (1987). *Women in educational administration.* Newbury Park, CA: Sage.

Smith, Dorothy E. (1987). *The everyday world as problematic: A feminist sociology.* Boston: Northeastern University Press.

Smith, Dorothy E. (1990). *The conceptual practices of power.* Boston: Northeastern University Press.

Spender, Dale. (1982). *Women of ideas and what men have done to them.* London: Routledge & Kegan Paul.

Spender, Dale. (1987). *Man made language.* London: Routledge & Kegan Paul.

Starratt, Richard. (1991). Building an ethical school: A theory for practice in educational leadership. *Educational Administration Quarterly, 27,* 185-202.

Villani, Susan. (1990). *A principle defined: The feminist attributes of leadership at work.* Unpublished essay.

Watson, James D. (1968). *The double helix.* New York: Atheneum.

Weiler, Kathleen. (1988). *Women teaching for change: Gender, class, & power.* South Hadley, MA: Bergin & Garvey.

Witherell, Carol, & Noddings, Nell. (1991). *Stories our lives tell.* New York: Teachers College Press.

Wood, Chip. (1991). Maternal teaching: Revolution of kindness. *Holistic Education Review,* 4(2), 4-10.

Wren, D. (1987). *The evolution of management thought.* New York: John Wiley.

Index